# Kinetic Drawing System for Family and School:

## A Handbook

*Howard M. Knoff, Ph.D. and H. Thompson Prout, Ph.D.*

Published by
**WESTERN PSYCHOLOGICAL SERVICES**
12031 Wilshire Boulevard
Los Angeles, CA 90025-1251
*Publishers and Distributors*

Sixth Printing ........................................................................ June 2000

International Standard Book Number: 0-87424-208-8

# ABOUT THE AUTHORS

*Howard M. Knoff, Ph.D.* is Assistant Professor with the School Psychology Program, Department of Psychological and Social Foundations of Education at the University of South Florida (Tampa, Florida). Dr. Knoff previously served on the School Psychology faculty at the State University of New York at Albany, and received his doctorate from Syracuse University in 1980. He has been a practicing school psychologist, a consultant to numerous mental health and school programs, and in private practice primarily with children and adolescents. His current research interests include personality assessment, consultation processes, and delivery of school psychological services.

*H. Thompson Prout, Ph.D.* is Associate Professor with the School Psychology Training Program at the State University of New York at Albany. Dr. Prout previously served on the faculties of James Madison University in Virginia and the University of Wisconsin at Madison. He received his doctorate from Indiana University in 1976. His experience as a psychologist includes school, hospital, and mental health settings. Current professional and research interests focus on therapeutic interventions, personality assessment, and mental retardation.

TO:


Tony Conti,
my mentor and friend,
"have a nice life"
HMK


and


Susan and Lauren,
who make my family drawing complete
HTP

# TABLE OF CONTENTS

# LIST OF TABLES

# LIST OF FIGURES

# FOREWORD

"I feel children's drawing is much useful to peep into their own mind. How do you think on these affairs?"

Professor N. Fukada, Doshisha
Woman's College, Kyoto, Japan

This charming quote from a recent letter sent to me by Dr. Fukada reflects an earthwide desire to better understand humans by "peeping into their own mind."

We humans understand very well how to peep into the universe and how to send people into space.

We understand very well how to peep into atoms and develop bombs which may destroy our earth.

We understand practically nothing about how to peep into the mind of the peeper. Unless we on spaceship earth learn to peep into and better understand the mind of the peeper, there may suddenly be an extinct race of peepers.

Notice that Professor Fukada finds drawings useful "to peep into their own mind." Most psychological tests using preformed questionnaires, pictures, words, or inkblots allow us to peep into the mind of the test developer but give a distorted picture of the individual's "own mind." Usually some theory, value system, philosophy, or bias is in the mind of the test developer.

I remember how, as a graduate student in psychology, I was startlingly refreshed to find a *blank* card in the *Thematic Apperception Test*. Murray, the TAT's creator, was daring enough to give the testee a blank card from which to project themes, actions, styles, and symbols from "their own mind."

B.F. Skinner, an avid spokesman for behaviorism, publicly disdained study of the "black box" (mind). Yet he devised a "tautophone" to produce meaningless sounds which the testee interpreted. The tautophone is a projective technique essentially using meaningless or "blank" sound upon which the testee projects meanings, symbols, and actions. Hopefully, some Skinnerians will stop focusing exclusively on outer behaviors and controls and turn some of their skills to much more needed inward study. Skinner's projective test, the tautophone, may be one tool for "peeping."

Freud developed a technique called "free association," which essentially consists of the analyst supplying a silent, safe, comfortable space, allowing the individual to project words into this silence. Perhaps the most revealing of these words are those recalled from the deep silence of sleep with accompanying dreams. Thus, free association is a projective technique allowing the individual to project memories, dreams, and symbols through words into the blank silence.

The "Quiet Therapies" of Japan—Naikan (Introspection Therapy), Shadan (Isolation Therapy), Seizo (Quiet-Sitting Therapy), and Zen (Meditation Therapy)—all use silence as a way to increase projections from within.

Kinetic Family Drawings (KFDs) were developed in the spirit of Murray's blank TAT card, Skinner's "tautophone" utilizing blank sound, Freud's "free association" projecting words into silence, and Japan's "Quiet Therapies."

The KFD examiner gives the "drawer" a *blank* piece of paper and says, "Draw a picture of everyone in your family, including you, DOING something—some kind of actions." There are two distinct advantages of the KFD approach: First, the test is relatively culture free and so the KFD can be used inter-, intra-, and cross-culturally. Second, it is very inexpensive.

My three books on KFDs are admirably summarized in Knoff and Prout's *Kinetic Drawing System for Family and School*. The KFD books were about growth in the family, defined as nuclear or extended by the drawer. The school is also a family in loco parentis and a child may spend more time with the school than with the nuclear family.

Knoff and Prout have combined the Kinetic School Drawing (KSD) with the KFD into a Kinetic Drawing System well suited to giving us a peek into the mind of the child growing or failing to grow in the school or family. They have done a thorough job in bringing together the KFD and KSD literature. While they have systematized and synthesized these two approaches, they have not lost the spirit of the original KFD attempts to combine science and art in a projective technique. Knoff and Prout clearly communicate and enhance the KFD and KSD approaches. The *Kinetic Drawing System for Family and School* provides an excellent source for those who wish to better understand the dynamics of self-growth in family and school.

Inventing a projective technique such as the KFD seems to me analogous to a person inventing, say, a telescope. The reliability of the telescope might be tested by having it placed and adjusted to see the moon, given certain atmospheric conditions. If, under these conditions, a statistically significant number of viewers reported consistently that they could see the moon using the telescope, the reliability of the instrument would be established.

Establishing the validity of what the viewer sees is a much more difficult problem. One viewer might see a man in the moon, another might see a woman. Some might report seeing heaven. Some might see the moon as yellow, others as white, and occasionally blue or gray may be reported. Some might perceive the moon as a crescent, others seeing it as round. Some might interpret the moon as bleu cheese, some even as Roquefort. Endless discussions in the literature might argue as to whether the moon is a yellow crescent-shaped man or a round whitish Roquefort cheese. Until someone lands on the moon and establishes the validity of such assumptions, the validity of the telescope will be in question.

If a relatively simple task such as validating the perception of the objective moon takes thousands of human years, the validity of what we perceive in the human mind may take much longer. As Professor Fukada so aptly said, our present psychological instruments give us only a "peep."

Because viewing the mind is so complex, psychologists are forced to start with clinical validity. Wise people who find an instrument giving them some "peep" of the mind may get together and see if common perceptions can "make sense" and continue a process narrowing hypotheses to a few which made "common sense."

In psychology, projective instruments are usually questioned and berated by the "scientific." Naive questions are sometimes asked in "validation" studies. In the KFD literature, someone has said that children using the style of compartmentalization show no significant signs of school disturbance as measured by teacher's ratings or "self-esteem" questionnaires. The conclusion drawn from such studies "invalidates" the KFD.

Having used KFDs for some 25 years and followed many children who chronically use compartmentalizations into adulthood, there are clinical observations and questions which suggest further observation and new questions. Clinical observation suggests that children who use compartmentalizations complain as adolescents that "people are invading my space." As adults, they frequently have difficulties "trusting" people and allowing them "into my space" which now includes "into my

life" or "into my house." Sexual "frigidity" may be one feature of a defense; that is, compartmentalizations are used to keep people from "invading my body." Fears and prejudices may come, such as "keeping strangers or foreigners out of my space."

I saw Diane the other day, a 34-year-old woman I have followed since adolescence in a KFD study. She has consistently used "encapsulation," usually a jump rope, in drawing her KFD self. Diane has had a chronic problem with obesity. She interpreted her own "jump rope" drawings as a wall built to protect herself from harm and unacceptable impulses. Diane does not like people to stand too close to her or touch her and has not had intercourse with her husband for five years; she keeps him at a distance. Protecting her space in a passive way was a survival mechanism begun early in childhood by Diane and continued into adult life. Diane was a "model" student in school.

What about a teacher drawn by students in a compartment or encapsulated? Why do they see this teacher as difficult to know? Why do aggressive children resent the distance and try to break through the teacher's compartment? Why do passive children in need of love withdraw energy from this teacher's classroom? How can we help this teacher come out of the compartment? What strategies can be devised by educators to help these children and teachers? Will these children do better in an "open classroom" setting or be fearful and withdraw in such a setting?

These are the kinds of questions that analysis of each KFD or KSD might pose to a thoughtful, informed viewer. Progress in the classroom could also be measured by the positive growth and freedom of the KFD or KSD self.

Thus, clinical validity serves as a beginning to ask more sophisticated and wise questions than "Is the moon made of cheese?" or "Is compartmentalization related to teacher's ratings of maladjustment?"

The Handbook developed by Knoff and Prout in creating the *Kinetic Drawing System for Family and School* gives us a powerful instrument to probe for questions and answers to more meaningful measures of projective test validity. Valid studies will come only when wise questions come from learned and observant "peepers."

Robert C. Burns
Seattle Institute of Human Development

# ACKNOWLEDGMENTS

The writing and production of this Handbook would not have been possible without the help and assistance of a number of individuals. We would like to sincerely thank the following persons for their contributions to this project:

Robert C. Burns, for his gracious Foreword and his pioneering work in the kinetic drawing method that serves as the foundation for our work;

Elvira Medina for her conscientious assistance with background research and her efforts in preparation of the drawings in the Handbook;

Maribel Gray for word processing the Handbook and showing us she truly deserves the title "Wang Wizard";

Dr. Robert Zachary, Gretchen Guiton, and the staff of Western Psychological Services for their efforts to improve the readability and organization of the Handbook and for their continued support and interest in our project.

Howard M. Knoff
H. Thompson Prout
June 1985
Albany, New York

# CHAPTER 1
## INTRODUCTION

### History of Projective Drawings

The use of drawings to assess children's and adolescents' feelings and perceptions—indeed, their personality dynamics and development—has an extensive history. The psychological implications of children's human figure drawings were first investigated in the late nineteenth century (Klepsch & Logie, 1982). From there, this field of study expanded to a wide variety of drawing formats with greater interpretive depth and detail. Goodenough (1926), whose works were later extended by Harris (1963) and Harris and Roberts (1972), investigated the normative development of human figure drawings from childhood through adolescence and related drawing maturation to intellectual development. Buck (1948), and later Buck and Hammer (1969), introduced and evaluated *House-Tree-Person* drawings, both developmentally and projectively, as manifestations of children's personality and psychological concerns. Machover (1949) detailed the interpretations of human figure drawings as reflections of children's self-concepts and/or ideal selfs. Also, Koppitz' (1968) developmental/projective scoring system and analyses of human figure drawings have been well regarded.

Child and adolescent drawings as personality assessment techniques continue to be popular in the field. Prout (1983) surveyed school psychology practitioners and graduate school trainers nationally on their most-used and most-emphasized personality assessment techniques. Practitioners' most used social-emotional assessment techniques were: clinical interviews (91% reporting frequently or always using), informal classroom observation (93% reporting frequently or always using), human figure drawings (83% reporting frequently or always using), and the *Bender Gestalt Test* (Bender, 1946) (72% reporting frequently or always using). The *House-Tree-Person* was used always or frequently by 63% of the practitioners, and the *Kinetic Family Drawing* by 62%. The trainers reported most emphasizing clinical interviewing, informal classroom observation, human figure drawings, and the *Bender Gestalt Test*. The *House-Tree-Person* ranked ninth and the *Kinetic Family Drawing* ranked twelfth in emphasis. Other professional psychology subspecialties have also studied and reinforced the importance and/or popularity of drawing techniques in personality assessment: Wade, Baker, Morton, and Baker (1978) in clinical psychology; Fein (1979) in clinical, counseling, and school psychology; and Goh, Teslow, and Fuller (1981) in school psychology.

Children's drawings of their families are included in the drawing and personality assessment domain. Initially suggested by Hulse (1951), children were asked to draw pictures of their families. These drawings were then evaluated as a gestalt, looking broadly at the tone and quality, and descriptively, looking at characteristics such as the size and proximity of figures and the differential pressure of line strokes or shadings. Hulse's technique became known as the *Draw-A-Family* (DAF), and this "nonkinetic" or "motionless" technique has provided important projective and clinical information. The DAF's directions, simply asking the child to "draw your family," however, often result in a rather "stiff," noninteracting "portrait" of the child's family. This portrait may restrict the depiction of dynamic family interactions, which might provide even more insight into the child's feelings and perceptions, and the family's role and influence with the child.

### Development of the KFD and KSD

To address the problems of noninteracting family drawings, Burns and Kaufman (1970, 1972) developed the *Kinetic Family Drawing* (KFD) technique, whereby the child is asked to draw his or her whole family *doing* something. The introduction of action into family drawings increased the diagnostic information available in these drawings both qualitatively and quantitatively. Thus, the KFD has significantly expanded the general depth of picture drawings as personality assessment techniques and, specifically, the depth of family drawings in this area. Burns and Kaufman's research has resulted in three descriptive and diagnostic volumes: *Kinetic Family Drawings (K-F-D): An Introduction to Understanding Children Through Kinetic Drawings* (Burns & Kaufman, 1970); *Actions, Styles, and Symbols in Kinetic Family Drawings (K-F-D): An Interpretive Manual* (Burns & Kaufman, 1972); and *Self-Growth in Families: Kinetic Family Drawings (K-F-D) Research and Applications* (Burns, 1982).

While the KFD investigated the interaction between children's psychological status and family dynamics and issues, Prout and Phillips (1974) investigated analogous interactions in school environments. This resulted in the

*Kinetic School Drawing* (KSD) in which the child is asked to draw a picture of relevant school figures (self, teacher, peers) doing something. Recent research with the KSD has included both qualitative (Sarbaugh, 1982) and quantitative analyses which have related the KSD to school achievement (Prout & Celmer, 1984).

## Purpose and Clinical Applications

Within the personality assessment domain, drawings as exemplified by the *Kinetic Drawing System* can be used in many ways: (a) as a sample of behavior which reflects a child's reactions to a one-to-one child-examiner situation involving semistructured task directions and follow-up questions requiring description, explanation, and elaboration; (b) as an "ice-breaker" technique which facilitates child-examiner rapport and a child's comfort, trust, and motivation; (c) as a technique linked to a clinical, diagnostic interview which moves beyond the action and dynamics within a drawing to more pervasive psychological issues and concerns; (d) as a projective technique which investigates one aspect of an individual's personality and attitudes; and (e) as a projective technique which assesses a child's perceptions of relationships among the child, peers, family, school, and significant others.

Aside from the personality assessment process, the *Kinetic Drawing System* is also a useful aid in child counseling and psychotherapy. The "state" nature of the technique allows monitoring of progress in counseling and presentation of psychological issues that are of current concern to the child. It is particularly useful with younger children and children who have difficulty with verbal expression. In an ongoing therapy, kinetic drawings are often used more informally with extensive use of inquiry.

This Handbook combines the KFD and the KSD into a *Kinetic Drawing System*, reviewing the current research and interpretation of both. Although these two projective techniques provide useful and important information separately, the *Kinetic Drawing System* emphasizes the advantage of using *both* techniques and of comparing the two differentially. Uses of the *Kinetic Drawing System* include: (a) assessing the pervasiveness of a child's difficulties across both the home and school settings; (b) identifying home/family issues which explain school attitudes or behaviors, or school/classroom issues that affect home behaviors (or both); and (c) isolating setting-specific relationships or interactions which contribute to the child's difficulties or may be available as therapeutic resources. The *Kinetic Drawing System* is also noteworthy in that its use is not restricted along rigid therapeutic boundaries. For example, although assessment of children's drawings is rooted in psychodynamically oriented theory, the *Kinetic Drawing System* is also compatible with behaviorally oriented assessment systems.

## Principles of Use

### Respondent Population

Although the *Kinetic Drawing System* is not restricted to a specific age group, the interpretive information is based on clinical and empirical studies using the KFD and KSD. The clinical interpretations of the KFD proffered by Burns and Kaufman (1972) include individuals between the ages of 5 and 20. Other studies of the KFD are based on more limited age ranges, usually within the elementary through junior high or middle school age levels. The KSD obviously is restricted in use to children of school age.

### User Qualifications

Despite its relative simplicity, the *Kinetic Drawing System* requires psychological sophistication to administer, score, and interpret. Its use should be restricted to individuals at or beyond the graduate level who are familiar with psychological assessment and visual-motor development in children of various ages. Accurate interpretation of children's drawings requires knowledge of normal conceptual, perceptual, and emotional development.

We must emphasize that the reading of this Handbook and the administration and scoring of a number of kinetic drawings *do not* certify one as trained and proficient in this projective technique. We strongly suggest that those who use the *Kinetic Drawing System* have appropriate academic training specifically in personality assessment and theory and in a mental health/psychological degree-granting graduate program. We further recommend that those who are "new" to projective and personality assessment and the *Kinetic Drawing System* find a supervising clinician to facilitate administration, scoring, and analysis until a mutually agreed-upon level of skill and comfort is reached. Only in this way can this technique and this Handbook be used efficiently and effectively, maximizing the benefits for referred children and adolescents.

The following chapters of this Handbook present the development and rationale of the *Kinetic Drawing System*, detail administration and scoring procedures, and provide interpretive guidelines. Chapter 2 describes the basic administration and scoring procedures. Chapter 3 provides guidelines for interpreting the *Kinetic Drawing System*. Chapter 4 provides illustrative case studies. Finally, Chapter 5 describes the respective histories and literatures of the KFD and KSD, including normative studies.

# CHAPTER 2
## ADMINISTRATION AND SCORING

The *Kinetic Drawing System* requires between 20 and 40 minutes to administer. Younger children often provide briefer responses and therefore take less time than do older children. Scoring and interpretation times will vary depending on the experience of the examiner. This chapter describes standard administration procedures and use of the Scoring Booklet. Four objective scoring systems developed for the *Kinetic Family Drawing* are presented in Chapter 5.

## Administration

### Placement in the Assessment Battery

In clinical use, the *Kinetic Drawing System* is usually completed in a face-to-face session with a referred child or adolescent as part of a comprehensive assessment battery. Depending on the referral problem, such an assessment battery might include an intelligence test (e.g., a Wechsler scale or *Stanford-Binet*), an academic achievement test, visual-motor assessments, adaptive behavior scales, objective personality measures, other projective techniques, behavioral observations, and clinical interviews. To date, there is no empirically determined order for techniques in an assessment battery to best elicit significant information. Thus, the placement of the *Kinetic Drawing System* in the battery reflects one's personal preference.

Naturally, we have our own preferred order of techniques when assessing a child's personality. After establishing informal rapport, we generally like to give an "ice-breaker" or "warm-up" test which is nonthreatening and minimizes anxiety. Often, we use the *Bender-Gestalt* (developmentally and/or projectively) or another similar visual-motor test (e.g., the *Developmental Test of Visual-Motor Integration*; Beery, 1982). Then, we give the intelligence test, because the child is "fresh" and this helps to maximize his or her performance. At this point, we also administer some of the projective techniques—for example, the *House-Tree-Person* (H-T-P), then the *Kinetic Drawing System*. It is helpful to place the H-T-P first because the child often draws the single figure required (i.e., just a house, just a tree, just a person) with no embellishments beyond those relevant to the desired figure. The *Kinetic Drawing System* then requires a more complex task (drawing interrelationships and actions) and a more detailed drawing. In a sense, the H-T-P's single drawings help the child to conceptually "lead up" to the more complex kinetic drawings.

A personality assessment battery often requires a second session. In the second session, any additional academic assessments and learning-oriented concerns can be addressed first. The rest of the personality assessment battery can conclude the second session—for example, the *Rorschach*, a thematic picture technique, the *Hand Test* (Wagner, 1983), an incomplete sentences technique, or a clinical interview. Note that we suggest administering the projective techniques toward the second half of an assessment session when the child's psychological defenses may be diminished because of increased rapport and trust with the examiner, increased relative fatigue, and decreased tendency to rationalize individual and group (family and school) dynamics and avoid significant issues. This placement of projective techniques, then, increases the potential for maximally significant projective results.

### General Administration Procedures

Within the *Kinetic Drawing System*, we recommend administering the KFD first and then the KSD. Very often, important family dynamics affect a child within both family and school contexts. For example, a child's self-concept is often primarily determined by his or her interactions with parents (and siblings), their attitudes toward his or her achievement and potential, and the identification process which occurs during the child's early years before school age. Additionally, the child spends many more hours within the family environment, and parents are usually the dominant and primary caretakers. By administering the KFD first, the clinician avoids potential contamination from the directions, drawing style and approach, and inquiry that may occur if the KSD were to be completed first. We like the KFD to be as "untainted" as possible so that significant family dynamics have the potential to be manifested. Other reasons for completing the KFD first are its more extensive research literature and its potential to provide more general information and dynamic insight into the child. The KSD, then, provides situation-specific information about the child in the school environment. Thus, the KSD can confirm the more general dynamics evident from the KFD and can address specific attitudes and interventions in the school setting.

Both the KFD and the KSD are administered in two phases: performance and inquiry. During the performance phase, the child is read the directions and produces the drawing. In the inquiry phase, the drawing is clarified by eliciting information from the child. Both phases are completed for the KFD before the KSD is administered.

## Performance Phase

The drawings are obtained individually with the child seated at a table of appropriate height. The child is given a #2 pencil (with eraser) and a sheet of plain white 8½″ x 11″ paper. The directions below provide a standardized set of instructions. However, the directions may be modified depending on the needs of the examiner. While the child is completing the drawing, the examiner can observe in a detached manner. It is often helpful to note such details as the order in which the figures are drawn on the page, the number and places of erasures, drawing style and motor dexterity, and other more global behavioral observations (e.g., impulsivity, planning strategy, facial expressions, motivation). No time limit is given; the performance phase is completed when the child indicates verbally or through gestures that he or she is finished. If the child refuses to complete the drawing or states, "I can't...," the child is encouraged to do his or her best with, perhaps, a repetition of the instructions.

**Directions for the Kinetic Family Drawing.** After providing a pencil and sheet of paper, the child is read these directions:

*"Draw a picture of everyone in your family, including you, DOING something. Try to draw whole people, not cartoons or stick people. Remember, make everyone DOING something—some kind of action."*

Remember that, when the child has finished drawing, the inquiry phase for the KFD is completed before proceeding to the performance phase for the KSD.

**Directons for the Kinetic School Drawing.** Immediately after completing the inquiry process for the KFD, the KSD is administered. Again, the examiner provides the child with a pencil and a second, clean sheet of paper and reads the following directions:

*"I'd like you to draw a school picture. Put yourself, your teacher, and a friend or two in the picture. Make everyone doing something. Try to draw whole people and make the best drawing you can. Remember, draw yourself, your teacher, and a friend or two, and make everyone doing something."*

Occasionally, children will comment about the KSD direction to include "a friend or two." It has been clini-

cally observed that referred, problem children sometimes say that they don't have any friends. While it is appropriate to encourage the child to make the drawing as complete as possible, the significance of such statements needs little expansion. The examiner should record any verbalizations the child makes while completing the drawings of both the KFD and KSD.

C. Burns (personal communication, March 27, 1984) feels that by limiting the KSD directions to including just "friends," there may be incomplete data in the drawing. Further, he questions including "make the best drawing you can" because this might increase such things as erasures and length of time for drawing in those children anxious about doing "their best." He suggests the following instructions:

"I'd like you to draw a school picture. Put yourself, your teacher, and two or more students in the picture. Try to draw whole people, not stick or cartoon figures. Remember, draw yourself, your teacher, and two or more students doing something."

As noted above, the instruction to include "friends" often yields significant clinical information about peer relationships; thus, we feel it is best to include this in the directions. The request to "make the best drawing you can" also adds a performance demand similar to that often associated with the school setting; thus, we recommend including both aspects in the directions. In summary, examiners should feel free to use the standardized directions for either the KFD or KSD, Burns' suggested KSD directions, or modifications of either set of directions depending on the child and referral concerns. Needless to say, the modifications would have to be considered during interpretation.

## Inquiry Phase

The inquiry phase occurs after the child has completed the KFD or KSD and after the examiner has taken the child's pencil away. The inquiry process attempts to clarify the child's drawing and investigate the overt and covert processes which affected its production. The ultimate goal is to elicit as much information and understanding about the drawing, the context, and the child as possible within the bounds of time and examiner-child rapport.

In the inquiry phase, the child should initially identify each human or animal figure with a name and age. Then the examiner should ask the child to describe what is happening in the picture and what each figure is doing. Beyond that, there are no rigidly determined questions or procedures.

The questions presented on the last page of the Scoring Booklet are *suggested* questions which have been adapted from other figure drawing inquiries. These can be further adapted and extended as the situation dictates. The questions may be asked in any order, and may be expanded to comprise part of a psychological interview. Some clinicians follow their intuition and the discussion's direction and uncover clinical information that exceeds the actual drawings in significance and importance. The suggested questions include the following:

1. For each figure in the drawing, ask the child that person's name, relationship to the child, age, and other meaningful characteristics or data.
2. Questions about the figures in the drawing include:
   "What is this person doing?"
   "What is good about this person?"
   "What is bad about this person?"
   "What does this person wish for?"
   "What is this person thinking?"
   "What is this person feeling?"
   "What happened to this person immediately before this picture?"
   "What will happen to this person immediately after this picture?"
   "What will happen to this person in the future?"
   "How does this person get along with other people?"
   "What does this person need most?"
   "What does that person make you think of?"
   "What does that person remind you of?"
   "How do you feel about that person?"
   "Do you feel that way about most people? Why?"
3. "What were you thinking about while you were drawing?"
4. "What does this drawing make you think of?"
5. Questions about the weather in the picture include:
   "What is the weather like in this picture?"
   "Is there any wind blowing in this picture?"
   "Show me the direction it is blowing."
   "What sort of wind is it?"
   "If you had drawn a sun in this picture, where would you have put it?"
6. "What happened to this family/class in this picture immediately before this picture?"
7. "What will happen to this family/school in this picture immediately after this picture?"
8. "What will happen to this family/school in the future?"
9. "If you could change anything at all about this family/school picture, what would it be?"
10. "Is this the best picture that you could possibly make?"

Ultimately, by means of observations and directly questioning the child, the inquiry process should answer the following questions. Note that, although these questions were devised for the KFD, many are also appropriate for the KSD.

What is your first impression? Who and what do you see? What is happening? How do you feel about what is happening?

What do you notice about physical intimacy or distance? Is the drawing warm or cold, soft or hard, pleasant or unpleasant?

Are people touching or are they shut off from each other? Who is facing whom?

How do the people in the drawing feel about their bodies? Are they using their bodies to show off? To hide? To be seductive? Are they proud of their bodies? Ashamed?

Who's ascendent? Who's descendent?

Are the "people" happy, sad, sadistic, suffering, blank, bored, rigid, strong, involved, detached, angry, subservient, trusting, or satisfied?

How does the group relate? Are they tense or relaxed? What are their messages toward each other? Do you feel love present?

Is this a family you would like to be a member of?

(Burns, 1982, p. 4)

Are the members of the group all engaged in the same or similar activities?

Are they doing something different? Is there total interaction, interaction between only a few, or complete independent functioning?

Is the family cohesive? Are the interactions constructive or destructive? Does there appear to be happy or unhappy manifest and latent content, respectively?

(Klepsch & Logie, 1982, p. 86)

Do visible actions agree with the child's verbal descriptions?

Are visible actions or verbal descriptions strange, unreal, or the expected?

Are self or other figures highly distorted such that without verbal description they would not be recognizable?

(Reynolds, 1978, p. 489)

## Scoring

After the KFD and KSD have been administered, the drawings are evaluated on a number of qualitative scoring categories. This qualitative information is integrated with the child's responses to the inquiry process for interpretation.

The Scoring Booklet (WPS Catalog No. W-208B, see sample in back of Handbook) has been designed for ease of recording, categorizing, and integrating the child's responses. It lists the five diagnostic categories used for interpretation (Actions of and Between Figures; Figure Characteristics; Position, Distance, and Barriers; Style; and Symbols) and their observable components. The clinician notes those components present in the KFD and those in the KSD. Space is provided for the clinician to record any unusual characteristics of each component. Additional space is provided for the examiner to record the child's verbal descriptions obtained during the inquiry phase. Thus, the Scoring Booklet organizes the child's responses. This provides a systematic guide to aid the generation and testing of interpretive hypotheses.

# CHAPTER 3
## INTERPRETATION

There are three levels of interpretation possible with the *Kinetic Drawing System*: (a) interpretation of the KFD and KSD, respectively, using the hypotheses outlined in this chapter; (b) interpretation of the general human figure drawing characteristics and variables discussed in the projective literature; and (c) interpretation of the *Kinetic Drawing System* in the context of the entire personality assessment battery.

Our approach towards interpreting projective techniques, including the *Kinetic Drawing System*, primarily involves a hypothesis-generating and hypothesis-testing model, rather than a procedure focused on differential diagnosis. We do not feel that projective techniques should be assessed "blindly" (i.e., without the benefit of background, interview, observation, or other assessment data). As noted in the specific *Kinetic Drawing System* interpretations in this chapter, any one drawing characteristic or variable could generate numerous interpretations or hypotheses. The clinician discriminates among the given hypotheses, choosing the most relevant based on his or her knowledge and understanding of the referral, the circumstances surrounding the referral, the child, significant people and environments interacting with the child (i.e., the child's "ecology"), and the relationship between the clinician and the child. Thus, the clinician chooses hypotheses to entertain and test further based on his or her knowledge and experience with the child.

After individual hypotheses are generated for the KFD and KSD, respectively, the clinician can then utilize the more general projective technique literature which provides general hypotheses for all human figure drawing styles and characteristics. Although a detailed summary of this literature is beyond the scope of this Handbook, many excellent references are available. The interested reader is referred to Ogdon (1977, 1982), Burns (1982), Buck and Hammer (1969), and Koppitz (1968). The clinician should use the same hypothesis-generating and hypothesis-testing approach with the generic figure drawing assessment as noted above with the KFD and KSD.

All hypotheses should be compared to each other and again to the clinician's knowledge and understanding of the child and referral, resulting in the identification of "personality themes." A "personality theme" is a behavior, reaction, attitude, or perception that consistently and

significantly appears across the child's *Kinetic Drawing System* analysis as well as across other assessment data. Thus, each personality theme is also considered a reasonable and realistic explanation of some facet of the referral or the child's personality make-up. Finally, a personality theme may represent one component of a child's personality trait, or it may be situation or referral specific (i.e., a personality state). A number of personality themes are likely to be generated from the *Kinetic Drawing System*. These should be intergrated and refined to provide a better understanding of the child and referral.

The identification of *Kinetic Drawing System* personality themes expands into the third (and highest) interpretive level as these themes are compared and contrasted across the entire personality assessment battery. Here, the clinician evaluates all available data, interviews, observations, and clinical impressions; makes a final analysis of the significant personality themes and interpersonal dynamics influencing the child and referral situation; and makes recommendations which logically address the analysis and interpretations. This is both an objective and subjective process, and operationalizes Strupp and Hadley's (1977) personality assessment philosophy quoted in Chapter 5 (p. 53).

### Interpretation of the KFD

KFD interpretations are separated into five diagnostic areas: Actions of and Between Figures; Figure Characteristics; Position, Distance, and Barriers; Style; and Symbols. These diagnostic areas, their general contents, and their interpretive hypotheses are summarized below.

One caution in interpreting the family drawings relates to children from different cultural and ethnic backgrounds. Some depictions of familial interactions may suggest problems within the family unit which, in reality, reflect "normal" family interaction patterns for certain cultural groups. Zuk (1978), in discussing issues related to family therapy, has noted that interviews with families of different ethnic and religious backgrounds yield different descriptions, partially based on the background of the interviewer. Similarly, examiners should be sensitive to different cultural and ethnic backgrounds and interpret the family drawings accordingly. For example, examiners should *not* immediately interpret depictions of family situations suggesting poor communication as necessarily associated with problematic interaction patterns; for some cultures, this may be the normative pattern. Thus, examiners should recognize their responsibility in ascertaining the presence and extent of cultural influences with all children they assess.

To generate KFD hypotheses, most clinicians will need to sift through the interpretation characteristics below for each KFD characteristic. This procedure will assure that all possible characteristics and variables are considered—especially when they may not be evident upon the first, cursory look at the actual drawing. Clinicians should recognize the theoretical biases inherent in some of the KFD hypotheses presented. For example, Burns and Kaufman (1970, 1972) incorporate some psychoanalytic theory and interpretation into many of their hypotheses. Each clinician must make an individual decision whether to utilize hypotheses which are at odds with their theoretical orientations or perspectives. This decision, however, is a common one evident in the clinician's

perspective of emotional disturbance, its analysis, and its remediation.

To facilitate the analysis of individual characteristics, Burns (1982) suggests that clinicians:

1. Take a global look at the KFD to assess its tone, overall quality, and glaring actions or emphases.
2. Focus on just the people in the KFD (fading out, in one's mind, the objects), and evaluating their interactions, expressions, and activities.
3. Focus on just the objects in the KFD (fading out the people), and evaluating their positions, emphases, and uses.

Characteristics of children's KFDs are listed in boldface type below. These characteristics correspond to those listed in the Scoring Booklet. In addition, interpretive hypotheses for each characteristic are presented, along with the source(s) of each hypothesis. The letters "CL" or "E" before each reference indicate whether the hypothesis is based on *clinical* (nonempirical) evidence or *empirical* data, although empirical studies obviously are also variable and subject to critical interpretation.

## *Actions of and Between Figures*

### Ball (e.g., baseballs/footballs being thrown between figures)
- Rivalry between the figures involved or separated by ball/ballgame (CL: Burns & Kaufman, 1970, 1972; Reynolds, 1978).
- Anger between or directed toward figures involved or separated; direct expression of anger when ball "thrown" directly at a figure; passive-aggressive anger when ball "misses" figure (CL: Burns & Kaufman, 1972).

### Large ball
- Desire to compete (CL: Burns & Kaufman, 1972; Reynolds, 1978).

### Ball directed towards a specific figure
- Desire and ability to compete with that figure (CL: Burns & Kaufman, 1972).

### Ball directed away from figure, or being held, or aloft in no particular direction
- Desire to compete with figure, but unable to (CL: Burns & Kaufman, 1972).

### Self not playing
- Jealousy towards figures playing with ball (CL: Burns & Kaufman, 1972; Reynolds 1978).

### Ball-playing isolated to one figure
- Difficulties relating to the environment, withdrawal tendencies, a "loner" (CL: Burns & Kaufman, 1972).

### Ball-bouncing with self or isolated to one figure
- Helplessness, inability, or daring not to compete (CL: Burns & Kaufman, 1972).

### Ball on the head
- Inhibition or inability to compete or interact with other (CL: Burns & Kaufman, 1972).

### Numerous balls on the head
- Identification of figure involved as the "center of attention" or a significant individual in the dynamics of the family (CL: Burns & Kaufman, 1972).

### Entire family playing ball together
- Associated with children willing to engage in constructive competitive activities (CL: Burns, 1982).

### Hanging or falling figures (e.g., drawing of individuals in precarious positions)
- Tension or anxiety (CL: Burns, 1982; Burns & Kaufman, 1972).

**Dirt themes (e.g., getting dirty, digging in dirt)**
- Associated with bad or negative affect or feelings (CL: Burns, 1982; Burns & Kaufman, 1972).

**Skin diving**
- Associated with withdrawal and depressive tendencies, usually in males due to an emasculating situation or person (CL: Burns & Kaufman, 1972).

**Mother actions**
### Cooking
- This is the most frequent action of the mother in KFDs and reflects a mother figure who meets the child's nurturing needs (CL: Burns & Kaufman, 1970).

### Cleaning
- This action is found in compulsive mothers who are more preoccupied with the house than with the people in the house. Cleaning becomes equated to acceptable or good behavior (CL: Burns & Kaufman, 1970).

### Ironing
- Usually found in the overly involved mother trying too hard to give her child "warmth" (CL: Burns & Kaufman, 1970).
- One of the "warmest" maternal activities, thus, great need for love and affection (CL: Burns & Kaufman, 1972).

**Father actions**
### Household activities
- Reading the paper, paying the bills, playing with the kids are frequent activities of normal dads (CL: Burns & Kaufman, 1970).

### Driving to or at work
- Usually found in fathers who are thought of in terms of abandonment or being outside of the family rather than an integral part of it (CL: Burns & Kaufman, 1970).

### Cutting
- Activities such as mowing the lawn, chopping, cutting, etc. are seen with "tough" or "castrating" fathers (occasionally mothers) (CL: Burns & Kaufman, 1970).

**High activity level (e.g., running, throwing, cutting, hitting)**
- Related to lower self-concept in the child (E: O'Brien & Patton, 1974).

**Father figure facing the self figure**
- Related to greater social and peer self-concept (E: O'Brien & Patton, 1974).

**Position of figures with respect to safety (e.g., figure in dangerous position [through visible or verbal description])**
- Indicates tension, turmoil, and anxiety (CL: Reynolds, 1978).

*Figure Characteristics*
*Individual Figure Characteristics*

**"Picasso" eye (single eye drawn disoriented on or in the middle of a figure's face)**
- Excessive concern and/or vigilance in relation to another figure or significant other (CL: Burns & Kaufman, 1972).
- Ambivalence and/or anger which is difficult to express toward another figure or significant other (CL: Burns & Kaufman, 1972).

**Jagged or sharp finger, toes, teeth**
- Anger, aggression, acting-out tendencies (CL: Reynolds, 1978).
- Fear of the figure—probably intense (CL: Reynolds, 1978).

**Long or extended arm**
### In other than self drawing
- A rejecting and/or threatening individual (CL: Burns, 1982; Burns & Kaufman, 1972).

### In self drawing
- Rejection of other individuals (CL: Burns & Kaufman, 1972).
- Need/desire for isolation or withdrawal (CL: Burns & Kaufman, 1972).

### Between two figures
- Indicative of a competition or struggling process for dominance (CL: Burns, 1982).
- Need to control the environment (CL: Reynolds, 1978).
- Insecurity (CL: Reynolds, 1978).
- Found in significantly more drawings of older vs. younger boys (E: Meyers, 1978).
- Did not discriminate an emotionally disturbed vs. emotionally adjusted sample of boys (E: Meyers, 1978).

**Shading or cross-hatching (scribbling or "blacking out" of a figure, or heavy shading [all except hair])**
- Found significantly more often in emotionally disturbed boys than emotionally adjusted boys; supportive of Burns and Kaufman (1972) interpretations (E: Meyers, 1978).
- Found significantly less often in younger vs. older boys (E: Meyers, 1978).
- Often-used style by middle-class adolescents (E: Thompson, 1975).

**Blackening of specific body part**
- Preoccupation with the body part blackened (E: Burns & Kaufman, 1970).
- Anxiety, perhaps about the body part blackened or issues around that body part (e.g., issues of sexuality when a body is blackened from the waist down) (E: Burns, 1982; Burns & Kaufman, 1970).

**General blackening**
- Indicates possible depression (CL: Burns & Kaufman, 1970).
- Identification of significantly interacting individuals in a particular family dynamic (CL: Burns, 1982; Burns & Kaufman, 1972).
- Attempts to control or deny an impulse (CL: Burns & Kaufman, 1972).

**Blackening an individual or object**
- Preoccupation and/or anxiety with, inhibition towards, or fixation on the person or object involved (CL: Reynolds, 1978).

**Body part "cut off" or occluded by another object**
- Denial or repression of the occluded area and an inability to "think" about these areas (CL: Burns & Kaufman, 1970).
- With boys, fears of castration in competition with father or older brothers (CL: Burns & Kaufman, 1970).
- Found in significantly more drawings of emotionally disturbed vs. emotionally adjusted boys; supportive of Burns and Kaufman (1972) interpretations (E: Meyers, 1978).

**Cutting off the head**
- Concerns or dealings with issues of control (CL: Burns & Kaufman, 1970).

**Presence of barriers between self and mother figure**
- Indicative of psychological distancing in high school adolescents (result not present for self and father figure barriers in the same sample) (E: Brannigan, Schofield, & Holtz, 1982).

**Omission of body parts**
- Conflict, anxiety, or psychological denial surrounding or including the missing part (CL: Burns & Kaufman, 1972; Reynolds, 1978).
- Dependency (CL: Reynolds, 1978).

**Omission of feet**
- Suggestive of feelings of instability or a lack of "roots" in the family matrix (CL: Burns, 1982).

**Omission of face in self drawing**
- Low self-concept and self-identity (CL: Burns, 1982).

**Transparencies (visible internal organs)**
- Distortions of reality, poor or tenuous reality testing (CL: Reynolds, 1978).
- For older children and adolescents, indicates possible psychosis, thought pattern disturbances (CL: Reynolds, 1978).
- Low IQ (CL: Reynolds, 1978).

**Drawing idealized picture of oneself (determined primarily through inquiry process)**
- Fantasy ideation or wish fulfillment (CL: Burns & Kaufman, 1970).

*Global/Comparative Figure Characteristics*

**Number of household members (number of figures in the drawing)**
   **Large family (in absolute numbers)**
   - Related to positive school and academic self-concept (E: O'Brien & Patton, 1974).
   **Large or greater number of siblings drawn**
   - Related to lower aggressive behavior in child (E: O'Brien & Patton, 1974).

**Relative height of figures**
- In general, size indicates the child's self-perceptions of importance relative to family members; the larger the size, the greater the importance or psychological influence (CL: Klepsch & Logie, 1982; Reynolds, 1978).

- Did not significantly discriminate emotionally disturbed vs. emotionally adjusted boys (E: Meyers, 1978).

**Small self drawing (relative to other figures in the drawing)**
- Poor self-concept, feelings of insignificance (CL: Klepsch & Logie, 1982) and inadequacy (CL: Burns, 1982; Burns & Kaufman, 1972; Reynolds, 1978).

**Large drawings (relative to other figures in the drawing)**
- Perceptions of power or aggressiveness in the individual drawn (CL: Klepsch & Logie, 1982; Reynolds, 1978).

**Self and sibling figures drawn relatively larger than parents**
- Related to greater aggression in child (E: O'Brien & Patton, 1974).

**Self drawing largest**
- Seen in 13- and 14-year-old middle-class female sample (E: Thompson, 1975).

**Mother figure largest**
- Seen in 17- and 18-year-old middle-class male sample (E: Thompson, 1975).

**Father figure largest**
- Seen in 17- and 18-year-old middle class female sample (E: Thompson, 1975).

**Similar treatment of figures**
- Similarity between self drawing and that of significant other (e.g., similar clothing, direction, facial characteristics or expressions) indicates feelings of admiration or fondness; identification with other individual; desires to be like that person (CL: Burns, 1982; Burns & Kaufman, 1972; Klepsch & Logie, 1982).

**Differential treatment of figures**
- Differential treatment between one figure and all others represented (e.g., facial difference, uncomplimentary pose) indicates familial rivalry (CL: Klepsch & Logie, 1982).

**Elevated self drawing**
- Child's striving for dominance or attention (CL: Burns & Kaufman, 1972).

**Elevated drawing of significant other**
- Perceptions of that individual's power or dominance (CL: Burns & Kaufman, 1972).

**Self figure facing away from other figures or facing into the drawing**
- Greater general self-concept (E: O'Brien & Patton, 1974).

**Crossing out and redrawing of an entire figure**
- Crossed-out figure may indicate the individual's true feelings or idealized feelings toward this person (or oneself, if drawing is of self) (CL: Burns & Kaufman, 1970).

**Omission of figures**
**Omission of others (failure to draw a significant other such as mother, father, sibling, or teacher)**
- Inability to express direct hostility with the missing person (CL: Burns & Kaufman, 1970, 1972; Reynolds, 1978).
- Family members omitted significantly more often by emotionally disturbed boys vs. emotionally adjusted boys (E: Meyers, 1978).

**Omission of self**
- Suggests a poor self-concept, feelings of being left out, and feelings of insignificance (CL: Klepsch & Logie, 1982).
- Indicates concern or poor feelings about or rejection of that person (CL: Burns & Kaufman, 1972; Klepsch & Logie, 1982; Reynolds, 1978).

**Inclusion of extra figures**
- Children often include significant people in their drawings (e.g., grandparents, aunts, other relatives) (CL: Burns & Kaufman, 1970).
- Additional figures may reveal disruptive influence protruding into the family (CL: Reynolds, 1978).
- Additional figures may reveal a closeness within the extended family (CL: Reynolds, 1978).

**Stick figures (where *all* figures are drawn as stick figures)**
- Defensive or resistant reaction to the test setting, especially when whole drawings are completed upon request (CL: Burns & Kaufman, 1972; Reynolds, 1978).
- Low IQ (CL: Reynolds, 1978).
- Use of regression as a defense mechanism if bright or older child (CL: Burns, 1982).

**Evasions (one or more, but not all, drawings depicting stick figures or no action)**

- Defensiveness, passive defiance, poor relation with the figure or fear of the figure (CL: Reynolds, 1978).
- Found in significantly more drawings of emotionally disturbed boys than emotionally adjusted boys (E: Meyers, 1978).

**Bizarre figures (e.g., robots, animalistic features)**

- Distortions of reality, poor or tenuous reality testing (CL: Reynolds, 1978).
- In older children and adolescents, possible psychosis, thought pattern disturbances (CL: Reynolds, 1978).

*Position, Distance, and Barriers*
*Position Characteristics*

**Placement of figures on the page**
**Drawing self next to significant other**

- May indicate that the child likes that individual, wishes to be closer, or wants more attention from that individual (CL: Klepsch & Logie, 1978).

**Drawing self significantly apart from others who are grouped in the picture**

- May perceive self as left out or not part of a group; may desire this apartness but cannot accomplish this in real life (CL: Klepsch & Logie, 1982).
- Emotional constriction, depression, lack of self-acceptance, rejection of or by the family, poor interpersonal skills (CL: Reynolds, 1978).

**Drawing of self between parents**

- Overprotected children or children desiring more parental attention (CL: Klepsch & Logie, 1982).

**Lack of interaction/integration of figures (no figure facing another, figures with backs or sides to each other, figures doing separate/individual activities or actions)**

- Poor communication or relating among the figures (CL: Burns, 1982; Burns & Kaufman, 1970).

**Parental figures individually not interacting with other figures**

- Rejection of child/family by parents (CL: Burns, 1982).
- "Tuning out" parents (CL: Burns, 1982).

**Rotated figures (rotation of self figure)**

- Feelings of disorientation within the family (CL: Burns & Kaufman, 1972).
- Feelings of being different with respect to other family members (CL: Burns & Kaufman, 1972; Reynolds, 1978).
- Need for attention (CL: Burns & Kaufman, 1972).
- Associated with feelings of rejection (CL: Reynolds, 1978).
- Neurological dysfunction (CL: Reynolds, 1978).
- Found more often in emotionally disturbed vs. emotionally adjusted boys; supportive of Burns and Kaufman (1972) interpretations (E: Meyers, 1978).

**Ordering of figures**

- Relative importance or self-concept within the family structure (CL: Reynolds, 1978).

**All family members in chronological order with figure size corresponding to each member's respective age**

- Typical response, indicative of little sibling rivalry (CL: Klepsch & Logie, 1982).

*Distance Characteristics*

**Physical distance between figures (distance between self drawing and mother figure, father figure, or other authority figure)**
**General**

- Distance between self and parent figures not related to psychological distancing as measured in high school adolescents (E: Brannigan et al., 1982).

**Close**

- Identification (CL: Burns, 1982; Burns & Kaufman, 1972).
- Need for attention (CL: Burns & Kaufman, 1972).
- Need for parental control (CL: Burns & Kaufman, 1972).
- Need for support and acceptance (CL: Reynolds, 1978).

- Emotionally disturbed boys tended to draw figures with greater physical proximity than emotionally adjusted boys; supportive of Burns and Kaufman (1972) interpretations (E: Meyers, 1978).

### Distant
- Feelings of isolation or rejection (CL: Reynolds, 1978).

*Barriers*

### Fields of force (a force or action between figures, such as throwing a ball, knife, airplane, etc.)
- Rivalry between the members involved or separated (CL: Burns & Kaufman, 1970; Reynolds, 1978).
- Highly competitive child (if the child drawing the picture is involved in the force or action), or perceptions of competition between the two drawn figures in real life (CL: Burns & Kaufman, 1970).
- Guardedness or defensiveness (CL: Reynolds, 1978).
- Drawn less often by younger vs. older boys (E: Meyers, 1978).
- Did not significantly discriminate between emotionally disturbed vs. emotionally adjusted boys (E: Meyers, 1978).

### The "A" syndrome or phenomenon (the presence of objects in a drawing where an "A" is embedded prominently [through shading or line reinforcement] in the object, and where the object is pictorially related to someone in the drawing)
- Need for school achievement or anxiety concerning academic progress and/or achievement (CL: Burns & Kaufman, 1970, 1972).

### The "X" syndrome or phenomenon (the presence of objects in a drawing where an "X" is embedded prominently [through shading or line reinforcement] in the object, and where the object is pictorially related to someone in the drawing)
- Attempts/need to control strong sexual impulses (CL: Burns & Kaufman, 1970; Reynolds, 1978).
- Presence of a strong conscience or superego (CL: Burns & Kaufman, 1972).
- Placement of the "X" may define/identify forces and counterforces in the context of a conflict (CL: Burns & Kaufman, 1972; Reynolds, 1978).
- May identify individuals to whom the child feels ambivalent (CL: Burns & Kaufman, 1972).
- Need to control aggressive tendencies (CL: Burns, 1982).

### "X" present in the legs supporting an ironing board
- Need to control or "be barriered" from sexual urges toward the person depicted ironing (usually the mother or mother-figure) (CL: Burns & Kaufman, 1970, 1972; Reynolds, 1978).

*Style*

### Line quality
#### Light, broken, or uneven
- Insecurity, inadequacy, fear (CL: Reynolds, 1978).

#### Heavy, overworked
- Anxiety, impulsivity, aggression (CL: Reynolds, 1978).

#### Unsteady, wavy
- Neurological dysfunction (CL: Reynolds, 1978).

### Asymmetric drawing
- Poor organization, impulsivity (CL: Reynolds, 1978)
- When accompanied by unsteady lines and faulty connection of lines or rotation of figures, indicates organicity (CL: Reynolds, 1978).

### Excessive attention to details
- Compulsiveness (CL: Reynolds, 1978).
- Insecurity (CL: Reynolds, 1978).
- Especially when accompanied by oversized or enlarged head, indicates preference for intellectualization as a defense mechanism (CL: Reynolds, 1978).

### Transparencies
- Low IQ (CL: Reynolds, 1978).
- Tenuous reality testing (CL: Reynolds, 1978).
- Accompanied by bizarre figure, indicates schizophrenic tendencies (CL: Reynolds, 1978).

### Erasures
- Ambivalence or conflict with figure/individual erased (CL: Burns & Kaufman, 1972; Reynolds, 1978).
- Reflection of actual vs. desired situation or vice versa (e.g., erasing and redrawing two figures closer together) (CL: Burns & Kaufman, 1972).
- Compulsiveness (CL: Reynolds, 1978).
- Insecurity (CL: Reynolds, 1978).
- Possible resistance (CL: Reynolds, 1978).

- Visual-motor deficiencies (CL: Reynolds, 1978).
- May not discriminate between emotionally disturbed vs. emotionally adjusted boys (E: Meyers, 1978).

**Compartmentalization (characterized by the intentional separation of individuals in a drawing by using one or more [straight] lines)**

- Children attempt to isolate and withdraw themselves (and their feelings) from other family members through compartmentalization (CL: Burns, 1982; Burns & Kaufman, 1970, 1972; Reynolds, 1978).
- Feelings of rejection by or fear of significant family member(s) (CL: Burns & Kaufman, 1970, 1972; Reynolds, 1978).
- Denial of, or difficulty accepting, significant feeling(s) (CL: Burns & Kaufman, 1970; Reynolds, 1978).
- Inability to communicate openly (CL: Reynolds, 1978).
- Younger boys tend to compartmentalize less than older boys (E: Meyers, 1978).
- Did not discriminate between emotionally disturbed and emotionally adjusted boys (E: Meyers, 1978).
- Often used by middle-class adolescents (E: Thompson, 1975).

**Compartmentalizing a significant other**

- Identifying a special (positive or negative) relationship, concern, or issue with this individual (CL: Burns, 1982; Burns & Kaufman, 1970, 1972; Klepsch & Logie, 1982).

**Compartmentalizing all figures (all performing separate activities)**

- Representative of a family that does not (or is perceived not to) do things together (CL: Burns, 1982; Klepsch & Logie, 1982).

**Compartmentalizing two or more figures together**

- Preoccupation with the relationship between these individuals (CL: Burns & Kaufman, 1978).

**Encapsulation (exists when one or more figures [but not all] are enclosed by an object's encircling lines [e.g., a jump rope, airplane, car] and/or by lines which do not stretch the length of the page)**

- Need to isolate or remove threatening individuals (CL: Reynolds, 1978).

- Found significantly more often in emotionally disturbed boys than emotionally adjusted boys; supportive of Burns and Kaufman (1972) interpretations (E: Meyers, 1978).
- Often used by middle-class adolescents (E: Thompson, 1975).

**Encapsulating two figures together**

- Close identification process between the two figures (CL: Burns, 1982).

**Folding compartmentalization (similar to compartmentalization above, but accomplished through folding the paper into discrete sections or boundaries)**

- Children with severe anxieties and fears (CL: Burns & Kaufman, 1972; Reynolds, 1978).
- Suggestive of acute emotional disturbance (CL: Burns, 1982).
- Suggestive of the presence of highly significant and disruptive interpersonal relations within the family (CL: Reynolds, 1978).
- Not found at all in a sample of 116 emotionally disturbed and emotionally adjusted boys (ages 6–14) (E: Meyers, 1978).
- Evident only once in a sample of 264 KFDs from emotionally disturbed and 162 from "normal" elementary school children (E: McPhee & Wegner, 1976).

**Lining at the top (lines drawn along the *entire* top of a drawing or above specific drawn individuals [could also include storm clouds or other objects drawn above figures] where *more than one line* extends across the drawing)**

- Presence of acute anxiety or a diffuse worry or fear (CL: Burns & Kaufman, 1972; Reynolds, 1978).
- Emotionally disturbed boys made more top linings than emotionally adjusted boys; supportive of Burns and Kaufman (1972) interpretations (E: Meyers, 1978).

**Underlining at the bottom of the page (occurs when *more than one line* covers the entire bottom of a drawing)**

- Characteristic of children from stressed and unstable families who need a strong foundation or sense of stability (CL: Burns & Kaufman, 1970, 1972; Klepsch & Logie, 1982; Reynolds, 1978).
- Found significantly more often in emotionally disturbed vs. emotionally adjusted boys; supportive of Burns and Kaufman (1972) conclusions/interpretations (E: Meyers, 1978).

**Lining and cross-hatching at the bottom of a page**
- Indicates a very unstable family and a yearning for stability (CL: Burns & Kaufman, 1970, 1972).

**Underlining of individual figures (occurs when at least two lines or repetitions appear under a figure or whole person)**
- Unstable relationship between child and individual, or between two individuals (if they are both underlined and "joined" or "connected" in the drawing) (CL: Burns & Kaufman, 1972; Reynolds, 1978).
- May appear in children whose parents are divorced (CL: Burns & Kaufman, 1972).
- Possible need for structure due to environmental dependence (CL: Reynolds, 1978).
- Did not discriminate between older and younger boys and emotionally disturbed vs. emotionally adjusted boys (E: Meyers, 1978).

**Edging (style characterized by having *all* figures drawn on two or more edges of the paper [e.g., vertically, upside-down])**
- Desire to be available or passively involved without direct interaction or involvement (CL: Burns & Kaufman, 1972).
- Defensive child who stays on the periphery of issues/discussions and resists getting involved at a more intimate or deeper level (CL: Burns & Kaufman, 1972; Reynolds, 1978).
- Child who is seeking structure and/or is dependent on the environment (CL: Reynolds, 1978).
- Emotionally disturbed boys made more edged placements than emotionally adjusted boys; supportive of Burns and Kaufman (1972) interpretations (E: Meyers, 1978).
- Evident only once in 264 KFDs (102 from emotionally disturbed and 162 "normal" elementary school children) (E: McPhee & Wegner, 1976).

**Anchoring (drawing all figures within one inch of a single edge of the paper)**
- Emotional constriction (CL: Reynolds, 1978).
- Environmental dependency, seeking structure (CL: Reynolds, 1978).
- Low IQ (CL: Reynolds, 1978).
- Related to visual-motor deficiencies and poor organizational skills (CL: Reynolds, 1978).

**Figures drawn on the back/other side of the paper**
- Conflict, usually indirect, with the individual depicted on the back of the paper (CL: Burns & Kaufman, 1972; Reynolds, 1978).
- Did not discriminate between emotionally disturbed vs. emotionally adjusted boys (E: Meyers, 1978).

**Self drawing on other side of paper**
- Psychological withdrawal or rejection of family (CL: Burns, 1982).

- Creation of "separate world" to take the place of family (CL: Burns, 1982).

**Rejecting a started drawing and redrawing an entire picture**
- Child is extremely threatened by the content or dynamics of the first drawing and redraws a "safer" picture in the second (CL: Burns & Kaufman, 1972).

**Perseveration or repetition of objects drawn in a picture**
- Obsessive thoughts (CL: Burns & Kaufman, 1970).

*Symbols*

The notion of interpreting symbols as concrete, second-order manifestations of a child's underlying or unconscious feelings or perceptions goes back to Freud and before. The clinician must be careful not to overinterpret symbols, but to use them in the context of the referral and data that are collected and known about the child. Some of the most common symbols are reviewed below with their possible interpretations or hypotheses.

**Balloons**
- Symbol of ascendence, need/desire for dominance within a family (CL: Burns, 1982).

**Beds**
- Placement of beds is relatively rare, and is associated with sexual or depressive themes (CL: Burns & Kaufman, 1972).

**Placement of all drawn figures in bed(s)**
- Greater significance of sexual or depressive themes (CL: Burns & Kaufman, 1972).

**Bicycles**
- Common activity depicted by normal children (CL: Burns & Kaufman, 1972).
- When overemphasized, reflects child's (usually boy's) masculine strivings (CL: Burns & Kaufman, 1972).

**Brooms**
- Recurrent symbol of mother figure which indicates figure's emphasis on household cleanliness (CL: Burns & Kaufman, 1972).
- "Witchy" mother figure (CL: Burns & Kaufman, 1972).

**Butterflies**
- Associated with search for illusive love and beauty (CL: Burns & Kaufman, 1972).

**Buttons (oversized or elaborated)**
- Associated with dependency or unmet needs; may be drawn on the individual looked upon for nurturance (CL: Burns, 1982; Reynolds, 1978).

**Cats**
- Ambivalence with mother figure (CL: Burns & Kaufman, 1970, 1972).
- Preoccupation with cats is symbolic of conflict or competition in identification/interaction with mother figure (CL: Burns & Kaufman, 1972).

**Circles (preoccupation with circular drawings or objects)**
- Schizoid personalities (CL: Burns & Kaufman, 1972).

**Clowns**
- Preoccupation indicative of children with significant feelings of inferiority (CL: Burns & Kaufman, 1972).

**Cribs**
- Indicates jealousy of (new) sibling in the family (CL: Burns & Kaufman, 1972).

### Heavy markings on a drawn crib
- A tendency toward denial or anxieties in relation to a (new) sibling/baby (CL: Burns & Kaufman, 1972).

### Repetition of crib drawing
- Preoccupation with the (new) sibling/baby's health and well-being (CL: Burns & Kaufman, 1972).

**Dangerous objects (prevalence of dangerous objects [e.g., hammers, knives])**
- Anger (when directed at a person) or passive-aggresive anger (when indirectly focused on a person) (CL: Burns, 1982; Burns & Kaufman, 1972).

**Drums**
- Symbol of displaced anger—anger which the child has difficulty expressing openly (CL: Burns & Kaufman, 1972).

**Flowers**
- Represents love of beauty or search/need for love and beauty (CL: Burns & Kaufman, 1972).

### Flowers drawn below the waist
- Feminine identification (CL: Burns & Kaufman, 1972).

**Garbage**
- Often found in drawings of children upset over the arrival of a new sibling (CL: Burns & Kaufman, 1972).
- Regressive and/or competitive behavior, often due to a new baby/sibling or new foster/stepsibling (CL: Burns & Kaufman, 1972).
- Associated with significant guilt feelings about rivalry or ambivalence toward (younger) siblings (CL: Burns, 1982).

### Figures taking out the garbage
- Associated with desires to take out the unwanted and "dirty" parts (person or persons) of the family existence (CL: Burns & Kaufman, 1972).

**Heat (e.g., suns, fires), light (e.g., light bulbs, lamps, floodlights), warmth (e.g., ironing, sunshine) objects/ depictions in drawings**
- Preoccupation/need for warmth and love (CL: Burns, 1982; Burns & Kaufman, 1970, 1972).

### Hanging lights on suspended chains
- Tremendous disturbance within a family, perhaps due to sexual issues or concerns (CL: Burns & Kaufman, 1970).

### Fire theme
- Often combines anger and the need for warmth (love) (CL: Burns & Kaufman, 1970, Reynolds, 1978).

- Intense and destructive tendencies, especially if needs for love are unmet or unresolved (CL: Burns & Kaufman, 1972).

### Electricity

- Great need for warmth, love, and power which may distort or preoccupy the child's thoughts (CL: Burns & Kaufman, 1972; Reynolds, 1978).
- Need for power and control (CL: Burns & Kaufman, 1972).
- Preoccupation with electricity indicates poor reality testing as in schizoid conditions (CL: Burns & Kaufman, 1972).

### Lamp

- Concern with love, warmth, or sexual issues (CL: Burns & Kaufman, 1970, 1972).

### Light bulbs

- Need for love and warmth (CL: Burns & Kaufman, 1972).

### Horses

- Common drawing by girls (CL: Burns & Kaufman, 1970).

### Jump rope

#### Self figure jumping rope

- Protection from others in the picture, from significant psychological interactions/issues (CL: Burns & Kaufman, 1972).

#### Figure (other than self) jumping rope

- Indications of significant rivalry or jealousy with that individual (CL: Burns & Kaufman, 1972).

### Kites (and sometimes balloons)

- Desire for escape and freedom from a restrictive family environment (CL: Burns & Kaufman, 1972).
- Kite-flying self drawing and proximity to another figure may specify the individual perceived as restrictive or punishing (CL: Burns & Kaufman, 1972).

### Ladders

- Associated with tension and precarious balance; proximity between ladder and figures may specify the focal relationship or interaction (CL: Burns & Kaufman, 1972).

### Lawnmowers (sometimes hatchets, axes, sharp instruments)

- In boys' drawings, theme symbolic of competition (usually with father) and concurrent fears of castration (CL: Burns & Kaufman, 1970, 1972).

#### Associated with self figure

- Competitive feelings, striving for dominance, attempts at control (CL: Burns & Kaufman, 1972).
- Wish fulfillment towards assuming a dominant role (CL: Burns & Kaufman, 1972).

#### Associated with other figure

- Fears or feelings of threat or competition from a dominant/dominating individual (CL: Burns & Kaufman, 1972).

### Leaves

- Associated with dependency; a symbol of that which clings to the source of nurturance (CL: Burns, 1982; Burns & Kaufman, 1972).

#### Collecting leaves

- "Collecting" warmth or nurturance or love from parents or significant others (CL: Burns & Kaufman, 1972).

#### Burning leaves

- Indicative of dependency needs not met, and the resulting anger and/or ambivalence (CL: Burns & Kaufman, 1972).

### Logs

- Associated with hypermasculinity or masculine striving (CL: Burns & Kaufman, 1972).

### Moon

- Associated with depression (CL: Burns, 1982).

### Motorcycles

- Associated with power, dominance (CL: Burns, 1982).

### Paintbrush

- Often an extension of the hand, and associated with a punishing figure (CL: Burns & Kaufman, 1972).

### Rain

- Associated with depressive tendencies (CL: Burns & Kaufman, 1972).

**Refrigerators**
- Associated with deprivation and depressive reactions to deprivation (CL: Burns & Kaufman, 1972).
- Coldness of refrigerator is opposite of the light or heat symbol (CL: Burns & Kaufman, 1972).

**Snakes**
- Phallic symbol indicative of sexual tension (CL: Burns & Kaufman, 1972).

**Snow (and other "cold" symbols)**
- Associated with depression and suicide (CL: Burns & Kaufman, 1972).

**Stars**
- Associated with deprivation (physical or emotional) (CL: Burns & Kaufman, 1972).
- May suggest pain, as in a comic strip (CL: Burns & Kaufman, 1972).

**Stop signs (also "Keep Out" signs)**
- Attempts at impulse control (CL: Burns & Kaufman, 1972).

**Stoves**
- Related to nurturance and oral needs (CL: Burns & Kaufman, 1972).

**Sun**
- Often seen in drawings of young children where it is stereotypically drawn and of little diagnostic significance (CL: Burns & Kaufman, 1972).

  **Darkened sun**
  - Associated with depression (CL: Burns & Kaufman, 1972).

  **Figures leaning toward the sun**
  - A need for warmth and acceptance (CL: Burns & Kaufman, 1972).

  **Figures drawn far away from the sun, leaning away from it, or faced away from it**
  - Feelings of rejection (CL: Burns & Kaufman, 1972).

**Trains**
- Symbolic of needs or perceptions of power, usually in boys, when exaggerated or accentuated in drawings (CL: Burns & Kaufman, 1972).

**Vacuum cleaners**
- Related to children with a history of oral deprivation or unmet dependency needs; as such, an intestinal symbol (CL: Burns & Kaufman, 1970).
- Symbolic of power and control; mothers using them are viewed as powerful or controlling figures (CL: Burns & Kaufman, 1972).

**Water themes (formation of water-related objects [e.g., ponds, swimming pools, oceans])**
- Fantasy ideation (CL: Burns & Kaufman, 1972).
- Associated with significant depressive tendencies (CL: Burns & Kaufman, 1970, 1972).

  **Figure floating in water**
  - Often the figure floating in the water is tied to or has significant depressive tendencies (CL: Burns, 1982; Burns & Kaufman, 1972).

## Interpretation of the KSD

KSD interpretations are also separated into the five diagnostic areas: Actions of and Between Figures; Figure Characteristics; Position, Distance, and Barriers; Style; and Symbols. Many KSD interpretations substantially overlap with those for the KFD. Thus, the clinician should analyze KSDs using *both* the KFD section above and the KSD-specific interpretations below. Most of the KSD-specific interpretations fall in the Actions of and Between Figures, Figure Characteristics, Style, and Symbols diagnostic areas; they have been generated primarily by Sarbaugh (1982) and Prout and Celmer (1984).

Given its school context, interpretations of the KSD should consider both the child's psychological and educational development and actual characteristics of the child's classroom and school environment. For example, regarding the child's developmental level, the KSD of an 8-year-old mentally retarded child would not be expected to be similar to the KSD of a typical 8-year-old. Certainly, the clinician must be sensitive to the interaction between one's "mental age" or developmental level and the diagnostic characteristics and variables evident in a KSD, which are "clinically" useful when compared to a reference group of a similar chronological age. This sensitivity should extend to all educational exceptionalities including learning-disabled, gifted, and behaviorally or personality disordered children.

If possible, the clinician should observe the child's classroom firsthand and get a good sense of the school environment. Sometimes, a child will draw a seemingly strange activity or object in the KSD. However, upon classroom observation or KSD inquiry, one may find this idiosyncrasy actually *present* in the environment. This characteristic, then, may become significantly less important and diagnostic. As noted above, direct observations and conferences will go a long way toward facilitating and crystallizing one's *Kinetic Drawing System* interpretations.

As with the KFD, the KSD interpretations in this section should all be considered, then accepted or rejected. The analysis of the KSD begins with the inquiry questions and discussion, followed by a formal, global analysis of the drawing and the people and objects in the KSD.

### *Actions of and Between Figures*

**Self figure engaged in academic behavior (e.g., figure engaged in reading, calculating, giving an answer appropriately)**
- Greater incidence of this activity significantly related to greater academic achievement (E: Prout & Celmer, 1984).

**Self figure engaged in undesirable behavior (e.g., figure inappropriately engaged in yelling, fighting, running)**
- Greater incidence of this activity significantly related to lower academic achievement (E: Prout & Celmer, 1984).

**Recess activity/actions (or other nonacademic activities—lunch, music, gym)**
- May indicate the best time/part of school for children having school difficulties; thus, avoidance or anxiety around the activities

### *Figure Characteristics*
*Individual Figure Characteristics*
  (See KFD interpretations above.)

*Global/Comparative Figure Characteristics*
**Number of figures in the drawing**
  **Large number of peers drawn (significantly greater than 2)**
  - Significantly related to lesser academic achievement (E: Prout & Celmer, 1984).

  **Lack of people drawn (or people represented symbolically by other objects)**
  - Probable avoidance of social interaction (CL: Sarbaugh, 1982).

**Relative height of figures**
  **Large self or child drawing (significantly greater than 49.25 mm)**
  - Significantly related to positive academic achievement (E: Prout & Celmer, 1984).

  **Large teacher relative to self drawing**
  - Feelings of inadequacy in school setting or with school activities (CL: Sarbaugh, 1982).

  **Large teacher drawing (significantly greater than 55 mm)**
  - Significantly related to positive academic achievement (E: Prout & Celmer, 1984).

**Characteristics of teacher drawing**
- This ambiguous figure must be analyzed by the clinician through characteristics in the drawing and the inquiry responses. The figure could connote nurturance, authority, academically oriented or achievement activities or issues, identification issues, or psychosexual issues (CL: Sarbaugh, 1982).

**Excessively detailed teacher drawing**
- Perceptions of an overpowering, dominating teacher (CL: Sarbaugh, 1982).
- Significant conflict between child and teacher (CL: Ogdon, 1977).
- Issues of authority or power significant for the child (CL: Sarbaugh, 1982).

### *Position, Distance, and Barriers*
  (See KFD interpretations above.)

### *Style*

**Transparencies**
- May reflect compulsive preoccupations with an aspect, characteristic, or relationship important to the child (CL: Sarbaugh, 1982).
- Indication of haste (CL: Sarbaugh, 1982).
- Poor reality-testing or looseness of concepts/reality (CL: Ogdon, 1977; Sarbaugh, 1982; see KFD discussion above).

**Emphasis on physical features of a room (e.g., emphasis on the building, classroom walls, furniture)**
- Need for structure, dependency on others (CL: Sarbaugh, 1982).
- Avoidance of social interaction (CL: Sarbaugh, 1982).

**Drawing viewpoints or perspectives**
  **Back views of people**
  - More common in KSDs because children often show the classroom from where they sit looking towards the teacher and blackboard (CL: Sarbaugh, 1982).

  **Bird's-eye view of classroom/drawing (KSD drawn so that one seems to be looking at the drawing as if far above, as if a bird flying over the classroom)**
  - Implies a sense of distance and social isolation (CL: Sarbaugh, 1982).

**Outdoor pictures**
  - Often drawn by children who dislike school, or who dislike its more academic aspects (CL: Sarbaugh, 1982).
  - Resistance to the task demands; situational to the personality assessment, child-examiner rapport process (CL: Ogdon, 1977).

*Symbols*

**Apples**
  - Dependency and oral needs (CL: Ogdon, 1977; Sarbaugh, 1982).
  - May symbolize school and teacher activities; thus, issues of nurturance and authority (CL: Sarbaugh, 1982).

**Chalkboard or bulletin board**
  - Contents/writing on them may indicate feelings/ anxiety toward academic achievement and self-adequacy in school (CL: Sarbaugh, 1982).

**Clock**
  - May represent order or structure, impersonal or teacher-specific pressures of time, or general awareness of time (CL: Sarbaugh, 1982).

**Principal**
  - Significant concerns or conflicts over issues of power, authority, structure, rules (CL: Sarbaugh, 1982).
  - May imply the need for a male identification figure generally or specific to the school environment (CL: Sarbaugh, 1982).

**School bus**
  - Avoidance, dislike, conflict of school activities (CL: Sarbaugh, 1982).
  - Serves to isolate the child from others (CL: Sarbaugh, 1982).
  - For a clear analysis, need to ask or determine whether the bus is coming to or leaving school and the child's affective reaction to either possibility.

# CHAPTER 4
## CASE STUDIES

In this chapter, the scoring, analysis, and interpretation of the *Kinetic Drawing System* is demonstrated through nine case studies of children ages 5 through 16. All the children in these case studies were referred for an assortment of learning and/or social-emotional problems.

Each case study is organized into six parts: (a) background information and referral, (b) observations during assessment, (c) *Kinetic Drawing System* reproductions and responses made during the inquiry phase, (d) characteristics evident in the KFD and their associated interpretive hypotheses, (e) characteristics evident in the KSD and their associated interpretive hypotheses, and (f) summary analysis of the *Kinetic Drawing System*, including a comparison of the family and school drawings.

The first four case studies are based primarily on the *Kinetic Drawing System* hypotheses and demonstrate report summaries specific to that technique. The remaining case studies demonstrate how the hypotheses can be integrated and reported within a comprehensive psychological battery.

## Case Study 1: Jason (Age 5-5)

### Background and Referral Information

Jason, age 5-5, was referred by his kindergarten classroom teacher for difficulty in readiness areas, including following and remembering directions, attention and completion of work, and fine motor performance. Since that referral, discussions have centered around Jason's poor relationships with peers and his general outward appearance as being a sad little boy.

### Observations During Assessment

Jason was assessed individually on two occasions within three days, with the *Kinetic Drawing System* administered on the first occasion. He came willingly with the examiner, but showed little affect. He rarely smiled, lacked spontaneity, did not care to make any decisions about activities, and made few attempts to build a relationship with the examiner. When he spontaneously brought in outside material, it typically involved aggressive activities (fighting, getting spanked, playing war with airplanes). Despite this lack of rapport, motivation during testing was acceptable and Jason appeared to work to

capacity. The assessment results, therefore, appear valid. However, his behavior during the assessment was unusual and, based on classroom observation, did not appear to be specific to the testing situation.

### Performance and Inquiry Responses

The KFD produced by Jason is shown in Figure 1 (p. 22). His KSD is shown in Figure 2 (p. 23).

**KFD inquiry phase.** (Q)*"It's mommy and daddy. They're walking in the house." (Q) "They're talking about nothing and they're thinking nothing." (Q) "They're saying swears. They're mad—they can't have gas for the car; the man wouldn't let them." (Q: Where's Jason?) "He's playing at a friend's house. They're making a jump for a bike. They have a dangerous bike—it could run over somebody and kill them. When you're not careful, you could kill yourself."

**KSD inquiry phase.** "I'm all alone playing—I want to play alone. I'm playing on the playground and I don't want anybody else to play. This is fun." (Q) "No teachers, no friends."

### Characteristics and Hypotheses for the KFD

*Omission of body parts*: Somewhat immature, but generally within expectations of Jason's developmental level (see Koppitz, 1968).

*Omission of self*: Suggests a poor self-concept, feelings of being left out, and/or feelings of insignificance.

*Placement of figures on the page (parental figures' interactions)*: Again, importance of him missing from the picture is evident. He perceives his parents as being involved with one another, but not necessarily in a positive or supportive way as evident from the inquiry.

*Lack of interaction/integration of figures*: Parental figures individually not interacting with other figures indicates poor communication or relating between parental figures; child perceives parents as not interacting or accepting him within the family system.

*Line quality (heavy, overworked)*: Here it is somewhat heavy with "scribbles" for hair above their heads.

---

*For all sections in this chapter describing the inquiry responses, the letter "Q" in parentheses (Q) indicates the point at which the examiner asked a question.

**Figure 1**
**Case Study 1 (Jason):  Kinetic Family Drawing**

**Figure 2**
**Case Study 1 (Jason): Kinetic School Drawing**

May indicate some anxiety or anger with the home environment. This again must be contrasted with developmental expectations.

*Other comments*: Presence of "belly button" in parental figures (but not in KSD) may indicate a dependent relationship with parents or a need for emotional nurturance.

## Characteristics and Hypotheses for the KSD

*Recess activities*: Especially with his inquiry responses, this may indicate that Jason is having academic difficulties at school and that he wants to avoid not only academics but his peers. The avoidance of peers may indicate some socialization deficits or anxieties, and/or some withdrawal tendencies.

*Lack of people drawn*: Again, reinforcement of hypothesis regarding avoidance of social interaction.

*Characteristics of teacher figure*: Absence of teacher figure is notable. One could say that Jason does not perceive the teacher as a potential support or nurturance system.

*Omission of body parts*: Same hypotheses as for KFD above.

*Lack of interaction/integration of figures*: Lack of any figures, other than inanimate, for potential interaction may allude to Jason's play development at the isolated play stage. This hypothesis needs to be assessed in the classroom and during recess for free play periods.

*Line quality (heavy, overworked)*: Consistent with KFD hypotheses.

## Summary Analysis and Hypotheses

Given the impression of Jason as "a sad little boy," his preoccupation with aggressive activities, and the *Kinetic Drawing System* drawings, it appears that Jason perceives a lack of parental acceptance, support, and nurturance at home.

Although he needs this nurturance, he may be afraid to ask for it because he fears that his parents will punish him for expressing these needs. Consequently, he has withdrawn from the family and has not had sufficient experience in interpersonal relationships which would allow him to interact positively with peers or other adults. Although he is covertly angry and deals with this through fantasy (the bike playing), outwardly he appears depressed—affectless, unable to make decisions, and uninterested in the examiner. At school, this depression is evident in his sad demeanor, lack of playfulness, and withdrawal from peers. In fact, he openly rejects initiatives from peers, preferring to play alone.

Recommendations included a parent and teacher conference to discuss and further validate these findings. It was also recommended that Jason be included in family counseling and a socialization play group.

## Case Study 2: Dustin (Age 8-9)

### Background and Referral Information

Dustin is a third-grade boy who is age 8-9. He was referred because of a learning disability and problems with social-emotional adjustment. Dustin has been on a special education plan for specific difficulties in reading and spelling since first grade, and has received speech (articulation) services since preschool.

Dustin was born in Mexico, came to the United States when he was 11 months old, and had a Spanish-speaking nurse until he was 1½ years old. However, he is not Hispanic; his parents' jobs brought them to Mexico. Dustin's parents divorced when he was less than 2 years old. Dustin lives with his mother and brother Chris (age 14-9) in an apartment, and they have had an assortment of female roommates who have helped to pay the rent.

Academically, Dustin has struggled in third grade. His learning disability is quite severe and it affects his motivation and self-concept. Behaviorally, Dustin acts out both at home and in school. He can be aggressive toward peers, both physically and verbally, and does not respond well to adult authority or direction. Both he and his mother have received counseling intermittently over the past two years.

### Observations During Assessment

Dustin was tested on six occasions within three months. The *Kinetic Drawing System* was given during the second session when most of the social-emotional assessments were completed. Dustin was a very friendly boy who developed excellent rapport with the examiner, and who usually showed good motivation and attention to assessment tasks. He understood directions quickly, and his answers were often clear and relevant. His greatest difficulty was in maintaining expected behavior during reading or reading-like tasks. He rarely got frustrated, but expressed his dislike through avoidance and silly behaviors. He could usually be restructured back on task, but sometimes required a more stern approach. Overall, Dustin's performance during testing was acceptable, and he appeared to work on the tasks with maximum effort and capacity.

### Performance and Inquiry Responses

Figure 3 (p. 25) presents Dustin's KFD, and Figure 4 (p. 26) his KSD.

**KFD inquiry phase.** The KFD shows Dustin's mother (who is pushing the tire to their car so that they can change the flat tire), Dustin, and his brother Chris (who can do everything academically and athletically that

**Figure 3**
**Case Study 2 (Dustin): Kinetic Family Drawing**

**Figure 4**
**Case Study 2 (Dustin):  Kinetic School Drawing**

Dustin cannot). According to Dustin, his brother is saying, "Dustin, get out of the way!" Dustin says, "O.K. Here comes Mom." Afterwards, Dustin added, "Look at Mom's picture—I made her funny with a long neck and she's so fat."

**KSD inquiry phase.** Dustin's classroom is represented in the drawing. The teacher is facing Dustin (who is facing away) and saying, "Read!" Dustin is responding, "I hate school. I want to play." Off to the side are Dustin's classmates who are saying, "We read O.K."

## Characteristics and Hypotheses for the KFD

*Omission of body parts*: The omission of body parts, including faces, indicates conflict and anxiety within the family system as well as a low self-concept within that system. It is interesting to note that Dustin drew a relatively negative, stressful situation for his drawing of his family doing something together. Further, he is being directed to stay out of the way by his brother, a potential area of conflict and/or competitive stress.

*Mother figure largest*: Mother appears as a dominant figure in the drawing. Dustin may see her as the authority figure against whom he is trying to rebel (note his comments on making Mom fat; in reality, she's quite attractive).

*Differential treatment of figures*: There is an indication of a rivalry between Dustin and Chris, in that Chris has facial features and Dustin does not; also between Dustin and his mother given the difference in their relative sizes.

*Evasions*: The tendency toward stick figures may indicate Dustin's defensiveness, passive defiance, or his poor relationships within the family; use of regression as a defense.

*Drawing self next to significant other*: Dustin's placement of the self figure near his brother may indicate his desire to be like his brother, a desire for more brotherly (male) attention, or an emulation. Interestingly, Dustin's response to his brother's "Get away" is not defiant but agreeable.

*Lack of interaction/integration of figures*: Poor communication with mother figure; perceptions of rejection by mother.

*Physical distance between figures*: Again, self figure drawn well away from mother figure.

*Line quality (unsteady, wavy)*: Poor self-concept; insecurity.

## Characteristics and Hypotheses for the KSD

*Self figure engaged in academic behavior*: Negative, evasive, rejecting attitude toward academics in general and reading specifically.

*Self figure engaged in undesirable behavior*: Predic-

tive of lower academic achievement.

*Characteristics of teacher drawing*: Perceives teachers as overpowering and dominating; significant conflicts between Dustin and teachers predicted; issues of authority or power over Dustin which he resists.

*Placement of figures on the page (lack of interaction/integration of figures) and physical distance between figures (distant)*: Reinforcement of conflict with teacher; perceptions of peers as a successful group yet a group which constantly reminds Dustin of what he cannot do (whether overtly or covertly). May indicate Dustin's intense desire to read, or not be learning disabled; feeling of isolation from peer group, or rejection.

*Line quality (unsteady, wavy)*: Reinforces hypothesis of poor self-concept, insecurity and inadequacy feelings.

## Summary Analysis and Hypotheses

Dustin appears to be expressing several unmet emotional and security needs, both at home and in school. At home, he feels ambivalent toward his brother—envious of his abilities and age, yet angry that he (Dustin) has so many academic problems and is not accepted fully by his mother. Dustin sometimes sees Chris as an identification or role model, yet this may be because he is the only other male at home. Dustin's relationship with his mother is also ambivalent; although he resists her power as an authority figure, he still needs her for security.

Dustin totally rejects school, academics, and reading as a positive influence or activity in his life. He sees his teacher as demanding something he cannot give (reading), and perceives his peers as able to do these academic tasks. He feels rejected and isolated from his peers and sees academic success as the only way to be accepted.

Overall, Dustin exhibits a passive-aggressive style and uses it to get attention, especially from his mother. He truly needs a close, supportive relationship, and some more stability in his life. He sees his family together only during negative or crisis times, and he requires substantially more nurturance and acceptance for himself, not just for his abilities or accomplishments.

# Case Study 3: Ellen (Age 11-8)

## Background and Referral Information

Ellen, age 11-8, is in the third grade. She is a native of Europe who has been in the United States since her early childhood. Her parents both died in an accident and she was sent to the United States to live with her aunt and uncle. She lived with these relatives for four years and was later taken out of the home due to emotional and suspected sexual abuse, primarily by her uncle. After a series of foster home placements, she was placed with a childless couple with the hope of adoption. This couple began to experience behavioral problems and outbursts from Ellen, and she was referred so that they could better understand and help her.

## Observations During Assessment

Ellen was very easy to get along with during the assessment. She was polite, cooperative, and very spontaneous. The assessment appeared valid and a number of important issues were later shared with her foster parents.

## Performance and Inquiry Responses

Ellen's KFD and KSD are presented in Figures 5 and 6, respectively (pp. 29–30).

**KFD inquiry phase.** "Everyone is eating out on tne deck. They're eating hamburgers—yesterday." (Q) "Ellen's saying, 'Yum, Yum—the food.' Don't know how I'm feeling. Mom's saying, 'I think I made a good supper.' Dad thinking, 'Maybe we'll mow the lawn.' I always help to set the table."

**KSD inquiry phase.** "The teacher is showing us how to do the project. I think I'm going to like the project—it's social studies. We're all going to work together on it. Let's get started."

## Characteristics and Hypotheses for the KFD

*Body part "cut off" or occluded by another object*: May indicate conflict over sexuality (note that Ellen is entering puberty while only in third grade, and she is "awakening" to boys) or over her ability to be more mobile or independent (cut-off feet).

*Bizarre figures*: Somewhat immature, but may indicate hesitation with accepting or being accepted by another foster family.

*Figure placement on the page (drawing of self between parents)*: Desire for more parental attention and stability of family system.

*Physical distance between figures (distant)*: Despite this desire, still a cautious perspective of the family as accepting of or acceptable to her. Also, feelings of rejection by other foster families which kept her "at arm's length."

*Line quality (unsteady, wavy)*: Insecurity with home environment; feelings of inadequacy that she "caused" the foster situations to not work out.

*Encapsulation*: Self figure encapsulated by chair indicates need to isolate or remove threatening individuals. This may be a self-protective mechanism so that Ellen doesn't get so close to these foster parents that she will be emotionally devastated (again) if she is "rejected" and sent to another placement.

*Circles*: Schizoid personality (but examiner doesn't feel this applies here).

## Characteristics and Hypotheses for the KSD

*Self figure engaged in academic behavior*: Interest and relationship to positive (or greater) academic achievement.

*Bizarre figures*: Self and peer figures appear to be drawn somewhat strangely—almost like "fetal" figures. Perhaps some indication of Ellen's sensitivity about being chronologically older than her classmates.

*Characteristics of teacher drawing*: Given the inquiry comments, seems to have a positive, supportive perception of the teacher.

*Placement of figures on the page (drawing self next to significant others)*: Desire to be closer to both peers and teacher; desire for more attention from these individuals/ groups.

*Physical distance between figures (distant)*: Need for attention, support, and acceptance.

*Line quality (unsteady, wavy)*: Insecurity, inadequacy.

*Emphasis on physical features of room*: Need for teacher/environmental structure, or dependency on others.

## Summary Analysis and Hypotheses

Much of the interpretation of Ellen's drawings is based on her childhood, its various traumatic events, her numerous foster home placements, and the transition to the United States and its school system and English-language base. Ellen is very ambivalent about her current home environment. Although she wants to be loved, supported, and accepted, she is fearful of another rejection which will take her once again away from a stable environment. Thus, despite her insecurity and feelings of inadequacy (she often blames herself for the previous unsuccessful home placements), Ellen is psychologically protecting herself by not getting too close to her current parent figures. This ambivalence may also include some needs for independence, which is typical of her preadolescent age-group, yet a feeling that these needs must be suppressed because they won't be acceptable.

The fact that she is age 11-9 also creates problems in school, where Ellen is in third grade with 8- and 9-year-old children. She is trying to adapt to this situation by "dressing down" and conforming to classroom rules and peer norms. Ellen feels she can be closer to her teacher and peers in school than to her foster parents at home, and wants greater acceptance and attention from them. She also feels that she can get more emotional support at school because there is less risk that she will be rejected. To summarize, at home, Ellen feels that she needs to demonstrate her ability to fit in and feels pressure because of this. At school, she can be more relaxed, work cooperatively, and share more of herself.

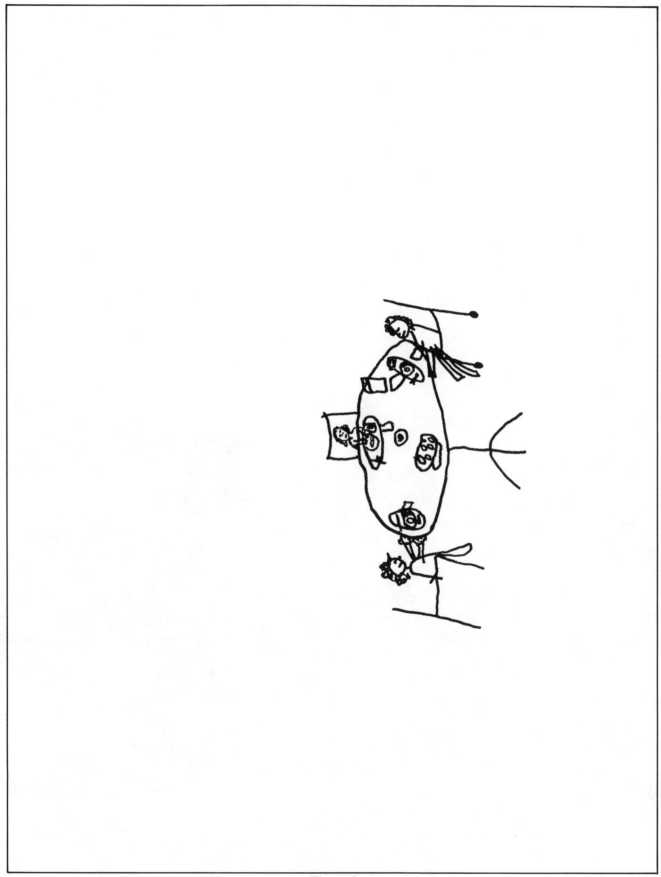

**Figure 5**
**Case Study 3 (Ellen): Kinetic Family Drawing**

**Figure 6**
**Case Study 3 (Ellen):  Kinetic School Drawing**

## Case Study 4: Kathy (Age 9-6)

### Background and Referral Information

Kathy, age 9-6, is a fourth grader. She was referred by her classroom and resource room teachers because of excessive school absences, a discrepancy between her potential and actual academic work, her lack of friends and resistance to any social interaction, and her attempts to get teacher attention through fantasy and pretending games. This referral is from a parochial church school.

Kathy's parents are both employed by the church school and live on the church's campus. Kathy's family had lived previously at another church campus, and moved to this campus when she was very young. She has a very young brother, Vinnie, another stepbrother, Ricky, who still lives on the first church campus, and a 19-year-old stepsister, Lisa, who lives with her. This is Kathy's mother's second marriage. In school, Kathy always wants to be in control of everything, and when not allowed to, she often withdraws, sometimes putting a "do not disturb" sign prominently on her desk. She also daydreams a lot at school and tries to buy friendship. Her "best friend" is a little girl in kindergarten whom she can control. Most of Kathy's absences are due to complaints of physical illness which have been checked out by the family doctor and found to have no physical basis. Kathy's teachers see her as "very unhappy."

At home, Kathy's father appears to be a very stern disciplinarian. Kathy was brought up surrounded by adults, and in many ways she has never been allowed to "be a child." She has always had responsibilities which were above her age level. Kathy's parents see her as very intelligent and use this to rationalize why her peers do not relate to her. Both parents have worked with the classroom teacher to help Kathy, and they were receptive toward the referral.

### Performance and Inquiry Responses

Figure 7 (p. 32) presents Kathy's KFD, and her KSD is shown in Figure 8 (p. 33).

**KFD inquiry phase.** Here, she did a lot of erasing and seemed very perfectionistic despite being told just to do her best. Halfway through, she asked if she could draw her cat. The entire drawing process took a considerable amount of time.

"That's me and that's my sister Lisa. We're getting ready to go to Maine to see relatives. I won't let my Mommy go on the trip—just me, and sister, and Dad. Dad's inside the house. Mom has to work on the switchboard. There's stuff falling from my suitcase—I'm a terrible packer."

**KSD inquiry phase.** "I'm showing my teacher a writ-

ten report about my cat Scooter. She likes it!! I'm going to get a good mark to show my parents."

### Characteristics and Hypotheses for the KFD

*Differential treatment of figures*: Good general self-concept.

*Omission of others*: Passive-aggressive hostility toward father; more open hostility toward mother. Significant negative feelings or rejection of parents and parental authority or style. Inability to express direct hostility toward parents.

*Drawing self next to significant other*: Desire to be closer or receive more attention from sister. Dependence on cat (or animals) for attention and psychological nurturance.

*Physical distance between figures (distant)*: Psychological distancing from parents evident.

*The "X" syndrome*: Ambivalent feelings toward father.

*Line quality (heavy, overworked)*: Anxiety, impulsivity.

*Erasures*: Insecurity with home environment/situations; ambivalent self-perception or self-concept.

*Cats*: Ambivalence or conflict with mother.

### Characteristics and Hypotheses for the KSD

*Self figure engaged in academic behavior*: Desire for or perceptions of positive academic achievement.

*Lack of people drawn*: Avoidance of social/peer interactions.

*Large self drawing*: Desire or potential for academic achievement.

*Large teacher drawing*: Positive academic achievement or achievement motivation.

*Characteristics of teacher drawing*: Positive attitudes/perceptions of teacher.

*Placement of figures on the page (drawing self next to significant other) and physical distance between figures (close)*: Reinforcement of positive attitudes toward teacher.

*Line quality (heavy, overworked)*: Lack of anxiety, good adjustment at school.

### Summary Analysis and Hypotheses

Kathy's drawings indicate some subtle and not so subtle conflicts with her parents and their parenting styles. Kathy seems to be having a greater degree of conflict with her mother than with her father, and would like to be able to control this relationship more (note that she "won't" let her mother in the picture go to Maine). Kathy is more ambivalent toward her father. Regardless, Kathy doesn't perceive her family as a supportive, integrated unit. Further, she rejects the home environment as

**Figure 7**
**Case Study 4 (Kathy):  Kinetic Family Drawing**

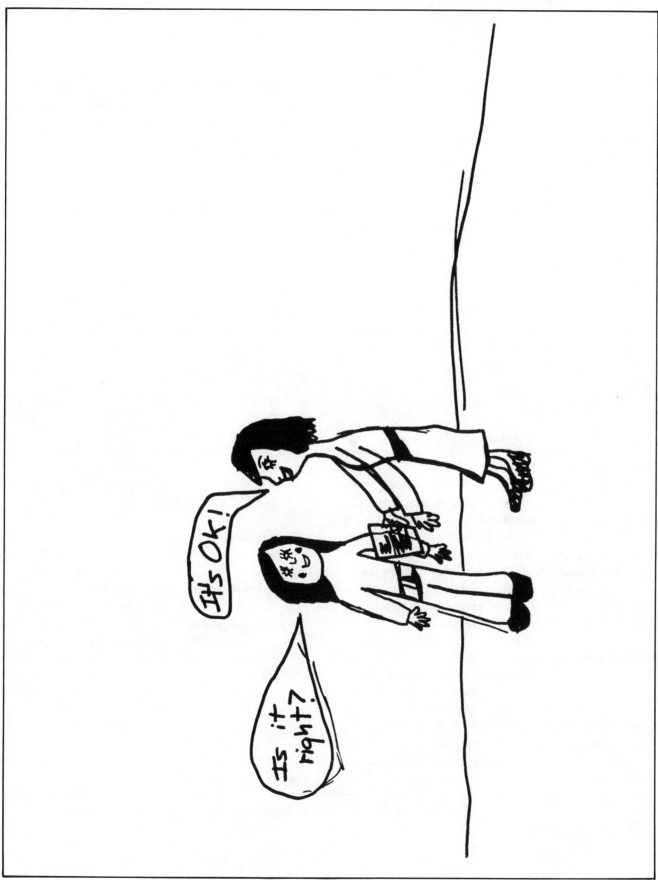

**Figure 8**
**Case Study 4 (Kathy): Kinetic School Drawing**

a foundation for the family unit, and instead appears to be "traveling away from" or distancing herself from this environment.

Kathy's perceptions of school are very positive and achievement oriented. As this is not the case in reality, this may be more of a desired or fantasized situation, or it could be an indication of the academic achievement that Kathy's parents are pressuring her to realize. A final hypothesis is that Kathy is truly capable of achieving and realizing her potential, but her actual nonachievement is a passive-aggressive response to her parents' pressure and the only way that she can control this particular aspect of her life. Nonetheless, Kathy's isolation and rejection of her peer group and its socialization experiences are significant.

Finally, it is also significant that Kathy includes her female teacher while excluding and rejecting her mother across the two pictures. Again, this may reflect Kathy's way to "get back" at her mother by accepting a substitute, or a fantasy situation which reinforces Kathy's need for an accepting person who will give her structure but not make unreasonable demands.

## Case Study 5: Kris (Age 10-0)

### Background and Referral Information

Kris is an attractive yet self-conscious fifth grader (age 10-0), who was referred for evaluation by her mother. Kris had difficulty passing her academic courses in fourth grade, and is continuing her poorer-than-expected performance in fifth grade. Her family experienced many "life crises" last year involving a number of close relatives, including the hospitalization of Kris's father for a heart attack and the death of a grandparent. Academic testing was performed to assess Kris's psychoeducational potential, in addition to a general personality assessment to explore her social-emotional development.

### Observations During Assessment

Kris was initially quiet and hesitant in formal assessment sessions and time was spent developing rapport and putting her at ease. She gradually was more spontaneous and was able to talk about her family and herself relatively openly. Projective testing was very successful with Kris; she enjoyed the tasks and exhibited little withholding of answers. Kris displayed a good sense of humor, but reacted negatively and self-consciously when complimented. Kris worked capably and with good motivation during psychoeducational testing. She enjoyed many of the tasks, and was aware of her successes and weaknesses. Overall, acceptable motivation and rapport were observed during test sessions, and the results appear to validly reflect Kris's current psychological functioning.

### Performance and Inquiry Responses

Figures 9 and 10 (pp. 35–36) present the KFD and KSD, respectively.

**KFD inquiry phase.** "We're all going to church. Everyone's happy—but Dad doesn't want to go. But it's a holiday (Christmas Eve). Dad's not Catholic, but everyone else is—not his family." (Q) "I want to get home and open presents. Katie wants to get home too."

**KSD inquiry phase.** "Lisa and I are helping the teacher. We're drawing and talking about horses. I love horses. . . That's all."

### Characteristics and Hypotheses for the KFD

*Hanging or falling figures*: Family or self tension or anxiety.

*Transparencies*: Distortion or poor reality ties.

*Relative height of figures (small self drawing)*: Poor self-concept; perceptions of family as having little psychological warmth, influence, or support.

*Differential treatment of figures*: Striving by Kris for attention or psychological support.

*Stick figures*: Use of regression as a defense mechanism.

*Placement of figures on the page (drawing self next to, and separating, significant others)*: Need for greater attention from mother; sibling rivalry.

*Physical distance between figures (distant)*: Need for closer psychological ties with entire family.

*Line quality (light, broken, or uneven)*: Insecurity, feelings of inadequacy at home.

### Characteristics and Hypotheses for the KSD

*Self figure engaged in academic behavior*: Desire or fantasy of positive academic achievement and relationship with teachers and peers at school.

*Shading or cross-hatching*: Possible depression, possibly across all settings, or specific to school and academics.

*Relative height of figures (large drawings)*: Relative to the family unit (and drawing), greater importance or psychological influence of school. This may indicate a pressure to achieve or a realization of her academic difficulties, or an environment that is safer or more secure and stable than at home.

*Similar treatment of figures*: Feelings of identification or desires to be like teacher and Lisa.

*Characteristics of teacher drawing*: Positive relationship or desire for such a relationship with teacher.

*Placement of figures on the page (drawing self next to significant others)*: Need for attention at school.

*Physical distance between figures (distant)*: Need for psychological stability which she hopes will be available at school.

**Figure 9**
**Case Study 5 (Kris): Kinetic Family Drawing**

**Figure 10**
**Case Study 5 (Kris):  Kinetic School Drawing**

*Line quality (light, broken, or uneven)*: Still, a basic feeling of inadequacy and insecurity at school despite these needs and desires.

*Chalkboard or bulletin board*: Desire to escape from academic concerns or achievement through fantasy.

*Horses*: Common drawing by girls.

## Summary Analysis and Hypotheses

Projective assessment with Kris revealed her above-average intelligence, good creativity, and the potential for appropriate academic achievement. There are indications of anxiety, especially around issues of homework and interpersonal relationships. Kris perceives a greater affinity with her father, aunt, and uncle, and manifests some worries about the recent hospitalizations in her family.

**Self.** Kris has a realistic sense of her abilities and seems comfortable with herself. She is happiest in non-academic settings, such as riding her aunt's and uncle's horse, but desperately wants a close friend. Kris avoids discussions about her academic record. She has some concerns about her family's health, but these are not neurotic or overwhelming fears and she wants to be included in any discussion of life-and-death situations at home. She appears to have handled her grandfather's death well, possibly because she was able to prepare herself. Currently, she appears to identify mostly with her father. Although this appears to be a long-standing pattern, it may be accentuated due to his recent heart attack and fears of a recurrence.

**Peers.** Kris does not have any friends, a gap which is filled primarily through fantasy. She feels lonely and isolated from peers, and somewhat inadequate at school (given her poor grades). This, in turn, makes her unsure of her social acceptance by peers. She is capable of relating and initiating relationships appropriately, but sometimes tends to withdraw. Her own positive self-concept does not generalize fully into peer interactions.

**Family and school.** These two systems appear to interact closely for Kris. She feels intense pressure at home to be successful in school. The pivotal issue appears to be homework. Kris identifies her mother as most dominant within the family, and feels the constant pressure from her to complete homework and perform academically. The result has been a power struggle between mother and daughter, with Kris withdrawing emotionally and creating psychological barriers. The main barriers—a tendency to regress into immature behavior and passive-aggressiveness toward mother—give Kris control of the situation and help counteract her feelings of powerlessness. Another issue here is Kris's anger with her mother about withholding information concerning family illnesses and hospitalizations.

Kris's need for more satisfying peer relationships is multiply determined. First, peer relations are important in that Kris can feel good about herself, forget the power struggles at home, and fulfill some of her emotional needs. In addition, she also needs an active support system in case she loses more relatives, including her father.

## Case Study 6: Robby (Age 13-4)

### Background and Referral Information

Robby, age 13-4, is a sixth grader in a middle school. He was referred for an intellectual assessment as part of his three-year special education review. Social-emotional assessment was requested to clarify some of the significant issues currently in Robby's life and his reactions to them. Robby has received academic support in the resource room and counseling support with the school adjustment counselor for several years.

Robby's developmental history reveals a number of significant stresses. Robby's mother divorced his father when Robby was approximately 2 years old, remarried him when Robby was about 8, and divorced him again two months later. Robby's mother then married another man, whom Robby especially liked; he unfortunately died of an infection when Robby was 10. Robby now lives with his mother and half-brother Aaron, age 3, in a trailer park. Robby's mother worries about his marks, particularly about whether he'll be retained, and is generally supportive of his counseling and resource room help.

### Observations During Assessment

With the examiner, Robby was somewhat tentative and interacted with little eye contact. He was polite, answered the examiner's questions quite completely, but admitted he was thinking about not coming for the evaluation. A reasonably good rapport was developed, and Robby appeared to take the tests seriously with appropriate motivation and consideration. This evaluation, therefore, does appear to be valid and to reflect Robby's current social-emotional status.

### Performance and Inquiry Responses

Robby's KFD and KSD are shown in Figure 11 (p. 38) and Figure 12 (p. 39).

**KFD inquiry phase.** "That's my cat Chico, my Mom, my little brother Aaron, and me. Mom is having popcorn, Aaron is dozing off, and I'm having something to drink." (Q) "My real Dad lives a few towns away—I never see him, but I'm happy about that because he always goes to bars and gets into fights." (Q) "My stepdad died suddenly—I really liked him; I miss him."

**KSD inquiry phase.** "I'm working on math with the teacher. She's gonna think I'm really smart—I'll do all the problems right." (Q) "The other kids are doing reading—they're being quiet."

**Figure 11**
**Case Study 6 (Robby):  Kinetic Family Drawing**

**Figure 12**
**Case Study 6 (Robby):  Kinetic School Drawing**

**Characteristics and Hypotheses for the KFD**

*Shading or cross-hatching*: Anxiety and strong indication of depression.

*Omission of figures*: No longer perceives father as a member of the family, nor his stepfather whose death he has psychologically accepted.

*Placement of figures on the page (drawing self next to significant other)*: Feels a need to protect his little brother.

*Lack of interaction/integration of figures*: Poor relationship with mother, poor communication—doesn't feel he can talk to her.

*Physical distance between figures*: Again reinforces hypothesis about his relationship with little brother; feels more distant or isolated from mother.

*Line quality (heavy, overworked)*: Anxiety about home and family environment.

*Encapsulation*: Close identification between two brothers; need to protect selves from mother.

*Underlining of individual figures*: Stressed and unstable family or home environment; a yearning for a strong foundation and sense of stability.

*Cats*: Ambivalent feelings toward mother; some emotional conflict over mother.

**Characteristics and Hypotheses for the KSD**

*Self figure engaged in academic behavior*: Greater potential for academic achievement, but this appears to be more fantasized than real.

*Drawing idealized self picture*: Fantasy indication or wish fulfillment specific to academic success.

*Differential treatment of figures*: Striving for attention.

*Characteristics of teacher drawing*: Perceptions of an overpowering, dominating teacher; issues of authority significant for Robby.

*Placement of figures on the page (drawing self next to significant other)*: Desire for more teacher attention and acceptance; perceptions of being left out of the peer group because of academic problems.

*Lack of interaction/integration of figures*: Poor relating to teachers and peers.

*Physical distance between figures (distant)*: Reinforcement of hypotheses for figure placement on the page and lack of interaction/integration of figures.

*Line quality (heavy, overworked)*: Anxiety.

*Encapsulation*: Fantasy figure utilized to remove threatening or anxiety-provoking thoughts, feelings, or situations.

*Chalkboard or bulletin board*: Anxiety towards academic achievement; fantasizes that he can do everything—including academics.

**Summary Analysis and Hypotheses**

Robby is concerned with a number of social and emotional issues. These issues are significantly affecting his attitudes toward himself and his environment, and have created a very anxious, depressed child.

Robby has a great need for both affection and security. His affective needs are almost infantile cravings for contact, most likely due to significant frustrations during his early childhood. These affective needs are poorly integrated into and dominate his personality. For example, Robby responded to one incomplete sentence blank with: "A mother *takes care of her child.*" Robby is still very much dependent on his mother's love and support. His security needs also relate to the family unit. He is afraid not only of losing his mother (she was recently hospitalized for emotional reasons), but even for the security of his home. For example, he responded to an incomplete sentence blank with: "My greatest worry is *when a truck rolls by—I'm afraid something will happen to the trailer.*" Both these affection and security needs are out of Robby's control (he could not control his parents' divorces nor his stepfather's death); thus, he feels helpless in the face of these real life events.

These realities have resulted in a number of other social-emotional reactions. Robby tends to withdraw from social interactions with both peers and adults, and uses fantasy as an escape mechanism. Unfortunately, even his fantasy takes on a depressed tone: Robby's person drawing from his *House-Tree-Person* projective drawings was an old, lonely man who lived in the alleys, was constantly drunk, and had walked the streets for 40 years. Interestingly, Robby enjoys science fiction books.

Robby's self-concept is very low indeed ("Sometimes *I hate myself*"). In general, he feels lonely, inferior, and socially rejected. He is very sensitive to being slightly overweight, and feels that his peers make fun of and abuse him physically ("I feel *a lot of pain inside me—kids talking about me*"). Thus, other than through some fantasy, Robby has no emotional relief either with peers or by having a good self-concept. It was not surprising that school rarely came up during the projective tests. Robby is dealing with so many other emotional issues that school is largely a secondary matter to him. These issues were so strong that they were even able to depress the scores on Robby's intellectual evaluation. Clearly, some of these issues need to be resolved before Robby can approach school in a free, unburdened way.

To summarize, Robby appears to be a depressed child who needs to work through some significant childhood issues. He is psychosexually immature, socially isolated, and has a *very* low self-concept.

## Case Study 7: Eric (Age 11-11)

### Background and Referral Information

Eric, age 11-11, is a seventh grader in a middle school. He was referred by the school guidance office for an evaluation of some persistent academic and behavioral issues. He failed two subjects during sixth grade last year, and although he made up one during summer school, he continues to show poor attention and motivation in his classes this year. Behaviorally, Eric has gotten into a number of fights with peers, and has spent considerable time at school in the suspension room. Particular issues to address were Eric's academic/intellectual potential; his view of the world, school, peers, and so on; and interventions that might be successful in increasing his academic motivation and social relationships.

Eric's mother was unaware of Eric's continuing behavioral problems in school this year. She and Eric live alone. She divorced Eric's father before Eric entered elementary school. She seems to recognize Eric's poor motivation, yet she allows a neighbor to encourage and supervise Eric's academics. Overall, Eric's mother realizes that she must provide more structure, but is afraid of its effects (e.g., Eric becoming angry and belligerent). She particularly noted that Eric is very adept at manipulating her and household rules, something that Eric stated spontaneously almost word for word to the examiner.

### Observations During Assessment

During the formal testing, Eric was somewhat fidgety, especially when working on tasks that required only verbal responses or open-ended answers. With visual tasks, he was able to attend well, sit appropriately in the seat, and work to his capacity. Eric has been previously seen by a physician for "hyperactivity"; the results were negative. He was quite candid during the assessment and interviewing, appeared to work to capacity, and understood task directions and expectations well. His attention seemed to diminish toward the end of the 2½ hour session, yet this did not appear to affect the results. Overall, it appears that the assessment did validly assess Eric's current social-emotional status.

### Performance and Inquiry Responses

Figures 13 and 14 (pp. 42–43) show Eric's KFD and KSD, respectively.

**KFD inquiry phase.** "It's my Dad, Mom, and me watching TV in the living room. We're watching 'Friday the 13th' and 'Good Times at Ridgemont High.' This is happening in Worcester when I was 3 years old." (Q) "Dad is happy 'cause he has his family. Mom's happy, too. I'm happy 'cause I'm doing things together with my parents."

**KSD inquiry phase.** "I'm the best basketball player on the team and everyone comes out to watch me play. I'm gonna score the winning basket—we're gonna win!!"

### Characteristics and Hypotheses for the KFD

*Long or extended arm*: Struggle between Eric and father for mother's attention. This may persist in the present (remember, Eric said the drawing is of him at age 3). That is, Eric may perceive his mother as still emotionally tied to his father, despite their divorce.

*Occluded or cut-off body parts*: Competition with father reemphasized (cut-off genital areas of father and self drawings).

*Relative height of figures (small self drawing)*: Feelings of insignificance, inadequacy within the family system.

*Placement of figures on the page (drawing self next to significant other)*: Close identification, desire for more attention from mother.

*Lack of interaction/integration of figures*: Poor communication among family members.

*Physical distance between figures (distant)*: Need for attention and parental control, as well as support and acceptance.

*Line quality*: Good line quality; somewhat immature drawing, though.

*Encapsulation*: Perception of close emotional ties between mother and father, or desire for a resumption of such close emotional ties. Perhaps this is a picture of the last time Eric felt in a stable and secure family environment.

*Anchoring*: Environmental dependency; seeking structure.

### Characteristics and Hypotheses for the KSD

*Balls (isolated to one figure)*: Helplessness or inability to truly compete academically (remember, this is his school drawing).

*Recess activity*: Best part of school day for a child having academic difficulties; avoidance of academic pressures and concerns.

*Self drawing largest*: Related to achievement, not necessarily academic achievement from this picture; need for athletic achievement and peer attention and emulation.

*Placement of figures on the page (drawing self apart from other figures)*: Perceives self as left out or not part of his peer group.

*Physical distance between figures (distant)*: Reinforcement of hypothesis for figure placement on the page.

*Fields of force*: Guardedness or defensiveness.

*Line quality (heavy, overworked)*: Anxiety.

*Anchoring*: Environmental dependency; seeking structure.

**Figure 13**
**Case Study 7 (Eric):  Kinetic Family Drawing**

**Figure 14**
**Case Study 7 (Eric): Kinetic School Drawing**

**Summary Analysis and Hypotheses**

Much of Eric's personality is dominated by his need for affection, attention, popularity, and (physical) accomplishment. Unfortunately, he is not satisfied with his own assessment of his abilities (he has a poor self-concept); instead, he depends on others to tell him how great he is. When peers or adults don't provide this feedback, Eric gets angry, does something to call attention to himself, and, when this fails, becomes aggressive and physically acts out. Eric wants to be a famous basketball player who has lots of friends, is happy, rich, respected, and is popular all over the world. Instead, he feels inadequate and frustrated by adult demands and structure, and he uses manipulation and force as the only way to control his environment.

Eric's home situation appears to be very inconsistent, providing him with many mixed messages. Because of inconsistent limit setting from his mother, Eric doesn't trust his environment and is unsure of behavioral boundaries. Thus, he tends to set his own behavioral norms, and becomes very angry and manipulative when others then force him to conform to their expectations. Eric particularly noted his ability to manipulate his mother (and others) so that he generally gets what he wants. Yet, he expressed his anger that "my mother lies to me and doesn't give me any allowance like she says."

Eric is not happy or psychologically secure with his current home environment. His KFD showed his mother, father, and him watching TV when he was 3 years old. Thus, Eric still fantasizes about times when "everyone was happy" and about having an intact family. In a sense, Eric *wants* the structure, rules, and boundaries that a 3-year-old relies on. At least then he might feel more protected and secure.

Emotionally, Eric has a significant need to be loved and accepted. In fact, there are very few relationships in which Eric feels any acceptance, except the relationships with his next-door neighbor and his grandmother. Eric worries a great deal about his relationships with peers. He thinks that his peers will accept him if he can make them laugh, be great in sports, and have things (money) to give them. When adults (or environmental situations) don't let him do the things that he thinks will let him accomplish these goals, Eric becomes angry, aggressive, and abusive. Often, Eric has misinterpreted what his peers really want for them to accept him.

Unfortunately, because of his dependence on others for positive feedback, Eric attributes few of his successes to himself. The only exception may be in sports, but here, Eric's success is more a fantasy that everyone will love him than a shift toward a more positive self-concept. Indeed, Eric appears to have few successes that would motivate him either academically or toward more socially accept-

able behavior. This would require substantial intervention involving the home, school, and mental health support systems.

## Case Study 8: Alan (Age 15-3)

**Background and Referral Information**

Alan, a ninth grader who is age 15-3, was referred because of his lack of participation in his classes this year and some recent behavioral incidents, including bringing liquor to school, a number of detentions, and numerous in-school suspensions which are bringing him close to an exclusionary suspension. Alan entered high school from out of state (New York) in the middle of the previous year, and failed his math and science classes for the remainder of the year. A preevaluation conference last year revealed no apparent academic problems. This year, however, questions about Alan's social-emotional status and the possibility of him functioning in the regular classroom prompted a formal referral.

An interview with Alan's mother revealed that Alan had previous academic difficulties in the late elementary school years, and that Alan entered a parochial school in sixth grade to provide more structure. Although Alan didn't like the rigidity of the parochial school, he did do better academically, appearing to be an average C student. Alan's family moved because "they were ready for a move." Alan's father is self-employed so the move was not financially motivated. The family had discussed the move previously. In fact, according to his mother, Alan was looking forward to it.

Since the move, Alan's mother reports that he has picked up the wrong type of friends, has had trouble with the police, talks about graduating from high school and returning to New York, and has had increasing conflicts with both his parents and brothers. Alan has increased his requests to sleep over at friends' houses, but on a few occasions he has left the house in anger and stayed out the entire night. Academically, his mother feels that Alan can do the work when he studies, but is unsure of his motivation for grades. Last year, he did not appear "visibly" upset about his failures. In fact, he decided *not* to go to summer school to make up for these failures.

An interview with Alan revealed that he didn't want to move, and that he does hope to graduate from high school. Many of Alan's detentions, according to him, are due to being late for class and fooling around in the hall. This quarter, Alan failed four subjects and gym, where he doesn't like to change into gym clothes and forgets them. Alan doesn't really know why he failed his subjects last year, and seemed to understand the consequences of bringing liquor into school this year. Socially, Alan doesn't see himself in one peer group, but feels that he has friends. Out of school, he does admit to some liquor and drug involvement.

## Observations During Assessment

During the formal assessment, Alan seemed to work to his capacity with appropriate motivation. He understood directions well, took his time in answering questions, and generally reviewed his work. On many of the verbal tasks, Alan would repeat the question or problem aloud before answering. This may have been a compensatory strategy when material needed to be accessed from his long-term memory. At times, Alan would say that he didn't know the answers. This appeared to be an evasive technique (he didn't want to take the trouble to formulate an answer) and he would usually try when encouraged. Overall, Alan appeared to develop an acceptable rapport with the examiner and, thus, these assessments do appear to validly reflect his current social-emotional status.

## Performance and Inquiry Responses

Alan's KFD and KSD are shown in Figures 15 and 16 (pp. 46–47).

**KFD inquiry phase.** "We're all raking the leaves outside. The kids are not happy; they don't like to rake, but they were told to or they won't get no dinner." (Q) "Dad is saying, 'Get to work!' I don't like this—I'd rather be at a friend's house."

**KSD inquiry phase.** "Everybody's playing basketball, but they won't let me play." (Q) "I'm sad and angry— if they don't want to play with me, I don't need them as friends. I'm going back to New York to live anyway."

## Characteristics and Hypotheses for the KFD

*Relative height of figures (father/mother drawings largest)*: Poor self-concept, feelings of insignificance, inadequacy feelings; perceptions of dominating parents, especially father; feelings of little influence within the family.

*Stick figures*: Defensiveness or resistance to the test setting; use of regression as a defense mechanism.

*Placement of figures on the page (drawing self next to significant others)*: Psychological identification with siblings over parents.

*Physical distance between figures (general)*: Distance between self and parent figures not related to psychological distancing.

*The "X" syndrome*: In drawings of children's bodies indicates conflicts between parents and children; need to control aggressive tendencies and resistance toward parents.

*Line quality (heavy, overworked)*: Tendency toward aggression; possible passive-aggressiveness.

## Characteristics and Hypotheses for the KSD

*Balls (self not playing)*: Jealousy towards peer groups; feelings of rejection.

*Recess activity*: Avoidance or anxiety around both academic and school achievement issues, and peer and socialization issues.

*Number of peers drawn (significantly greater than 2)*: Indications of academic achievement problems.

*Stick figures*: Use of regression as a defense mechanism.

*Placement of figures on the page (self significantly apart from others)*: Perceptions of being "left out" of the peer group, or desires to be left out or a loner.

*Physical distance between figures (general)*: No relationship between proximity and psychological distancing.

*Line quality (heavy, overworked)*: Aggressive tendencies, anger (at being left out).

## Summary Analysis and Hypotheses

The test results indicate a number of significant issues that are affecting Alan's social-emotional life, and may give some insights into his problematic behaviors. Many of these issues revolve around his feelings of powerlessness. Alan is currently overreacting to a fairly typical adolescent concern that everyone in his life, except himself, is controlling his every move. This concern seems to have been present for a number of years, however. For example, Alan was placed in parochial school when he was unable to achieve academically and set limits for himself. At this time, Alan is focusing on his "forced" move to his new community. Because every bad thing that happens or that he does now can be blamed on that, Alan absolves himself of any and all responsibilities. Meanwhile, he is fighting his perceived sense of powerlessness in a passive-aggressive manner. His anger is not expressed overtly as much as in a passive way by not working to his capacity in school, bringing alcohol to school, troubles with the police, and drug involvement. These passive-aggressive behaviors allow Alan to control his environment: No one can force him to change them if he doesn't want to.

Alan's academic difficulties pose another area in which he feels powerless. Alan *does* need academic support, and does realize that he doesn't achieve as well as his peers. Yet, Alan doesn't have control of either the way that he learns or the ways to get the help that he may need. Alan's reaction is to not try academically, passively say that he doesn't know why he fails, and state that he could achieve if he wanted to. (Incidently, his decision not to go to summer school was probably a good one; Alan most likely escaped another failure experience.)

Much of Alan's anger is more actively focused at

**Figure 15**
**Case Study 8 (Alan):  Kinetic Family Drawing**

**Figure 16**
**Case Study 8 (Alan): Kinetic School Drawing**

home. When asked to draw his family doing something together, Alan said, "Huh? I don't want to do *that*." Alan is currently rejecting his family as a supportive unit. He rejects his parents as authority figures, expecting them to dominate and control his comings and goings. When too much pressure exists at home, Alan either asks to spend nights over at friends' houses or takes control of his life by leaving without permission.

Many of the current family conflicts revolve around things that Alan wants—whether tangible items or privileges. Alan has a distinct need to attain goals and privileges that *he* wants. This reflects his significant emotional immaturity, and sometimes a lack of understanding and contact with his environment. Although he wants these goals, Alan either does not know how to attain them on his own, or does not want to invest the necessary physical and psychological energy. Thus, Alan expects his environment to give him what he wants.

He rejects his family as a support system, and has turned to peers to take up the slack. Unfortunately, this support system is less of an interpersonal support system, and more of an escape mechanism channeled into near-delinquent acts and drug involvement. Alan is currently using fantasy and drugs to not only escape from his perceived pressures, but again as a way that he can control his life. Adult support systems are also rejected by Alan. He appears very suspicious of his environment and is not willing to enter into another relationship that may require either an emotional investment or another possible loss of control.

Alan has no real plans or goals at this time. He is very caught up in his struggle with control issues, and spends much of his time passively resisting his environment and its demands. He is currently unable to make decisions on how to work with his environment or take responsibility—on a reality level—for changing and moving ahead.

## Case Study 9: Jackie (Age 16-5)

### Background and Referral Information

Jackie, age 16-5, is in the eleventh grade. She was referred by her parents for a psychological examination to evaluate some of her recent feelings and behaviors and to determine an appropriate course of action. Jackie's father was interviewed, and psychological testing with Jackie was completed later that day.

Jackie has had a relatively unstable, emotionally laden school history. She has had extreme difficulties relating with peers, has rarely developed positive and motivating relationships with her teachers, and has experienced feelings of both academic and emotional rejection

at school. Jackie feels that she can accomplish anything she puts her mind to, but desires teachers who are friendly and to whom she can relate, and smaller (more secure) classes.

At home, both Jackie's parents have made major vocational changes in the past two years. This necessitates the father's absence during most of the week, and the mother's attention has been focused more on her studies than on the two children. Jackie has a brother one year older, but there is little supportive interaction between them.

Jackie's social-emotional history is further complicated by (according to her) at least two rapes. One occurred when Jackie accepted a ride from two men who later attacked her. Jackie didn't press charges in this instance. Another rape occurred after Jackie had run away from home. According to Jackie, this was a particularly vicious rape which scared her mostly because she wasn't in control of the situation.

Jackie is now being supervised by a state program. She was recently placed in a foster home program after an altercation with her mother. Socially, Jackie appears to interact with an older peer group, be involved at least with alcohol, and be sexually promiscuous, and yet wishes she were accepted more by her same-aged peers.

### Observations During Assessment

During the assessment session, Jackie was initially tentative but developed a good rapport over time. She expressed concerns and fears about her recent behavior, and yet had little insight into why it occurred. She worried about her sexual feelings, and expressed some anxiety about becoming pregnant. Jackie appeared coherent and reality-oriented, and seemed to take the assessment session seriously.

### Performance and Inquiry Responses

Jackie's KFD is shown in Figure 17 (p. 49), and her KSD in Figure 18 (p. 50).

**KFD inquiry phase.** "Everybody is at the table eating. Last time this happened was a while ago—a week ago last Sunday. Dad has a *lot* of food, but Mom only has a little—she always takes too little to eat. I have a good amount."

**KSD inquiry phase.** "We're in English class and they're reading a novel. It's really boring—*A Tale of Two Cities*. The teacher just asked me a question—Ha! I'm asleep. I didn't know the answer anyway."

### Characteristics and Hypotheses for the KFD

*Hanging or falling figures*: Tension or anxiety.
*Father actions (father figure facing self figure)*: Father negative (facial) attitude toward Jackie is appar-

**Figure 17**
**Case Study 9 (Jackie): Kinetic Family Drawing**

**Figure 18**
**Case Study 9 (Jackie): Kinetic School Drawing**

ent despite hypothesis of greater social and peer self-concept.

*Position of figures with respect to safety*: Tension, turmoil, and anxiety within the family.

*Shading or cross-hatching*: Possible depression among children.

*Occluded or cut-off body parts*: Concerns with issues of control; need for psychological distancing.

*Omission of body parts*: Conflict, anxiety; low self-concept and lack of self-identity.

*Differential treatment of figures*: Familial rivalry; perceptions of parental, especially father's, power or dominance.

*Lack of interaction/integration of figures*: Poor communicating or relating among family members; "tuning out" by children.

*Physical distance between figures (general)*: No relationship between proximity and psychological distancing.

*Fields of force*: Rivalry between family members; guardedness or defensiveness; highly competitive child within the family vying for attention.

*Line quality (light, broken, or uneven)*: Insecurity, inadequacy.

*Circles*: Schizoid personalities.

## Characteristics and Hypotheses for the KSD

*Self figure engaged in undesirable behavior*: Greater probability of lower academic achievement.

*Shading or cross-hatching*: Anxiety around academic achievement.

*Occluded or cut-off body parts*: Concerns with issues of control and authority.

*Omission of body parts*: Low self-concept and lack of self-identity within a school or academic context.

*Differential treatment of figures*: Perceptions of teacher as dominant and powerful.

*Relative height of figures (large teacher relative to self drawing)*: Feelings of inadequacy in the school setting.

*Characteristics of teacher drawing*: Perceptions of teacher as dominant, demanding, and negative toward her.

*Placement of figures on the page (self drawn apart from others)*: Perceives self as left out or not part of a group; desires more peer or academic acceptance; poor socialization or interpersonal skills; depression; feels rejected by peers.

*Lack of interaction/integration of figures*: Poor relating to academic situations or peers; "tunes out" school and academics.

*Physical distance between figures (general)*: No relationship to psychological distancing.

*Line quality (light, broken, or uneven)*: Insecurity; feelings of inadequacy at school.

*Bird's-eye view of classroom*: Implies a sense of distance and social isolation.

## Summary Analysis and Hypotheses

Clinically, Jackie manifests a chronic character disorder in which passive-aggressive elements dominate her behavior. Jackie may appear relatively well defended and in little psychological distress, yet she is repressing feelings of insecurity, anger, and anxiety. Jackie is likely to manifest severe periods of impulsive acting-out followed by periods of inhibition and constraint. Jackie has relatively little self-insight, and while she may resolve to be "good," these resolutions are generally short-lived.

Jackie is harboring feelings resulting from (in her view) an unsupportive home with a frequently absent yet dominating father, psychosexual conflict resulting from childhood traumas and her two (or more) recent rapes, and a fear of her own behavior and future. Jackie reacts to these feelings by blaming others, using passive-aggressive manipulation, and ultimately by impulsively running from her stresses. Jackie perceives these stresses as environmentally bound; she is unable to understand specifically why and how she feels. She has a high tolerance for these pressures, but when they exceed her frustration level, she acts egocentrically and antisocially. Unfortunately, Jackie does not learn from her previous experiences. Thus, this behavior pattern is likely to continue.

Jackie's clinical pattern is often associated with significant needs for social approval, sexual promiscuity and maladjustment, alcohol and other drug abuse, and some depression. Jackie has average to above-average intelligence, but it is currently focused on her emotional needs. Jackie exhibits some suicidal ideation, but this is most likely to manifest itself in situations where she is victimized by others (being raped) or engages in long-term self-destructive behavior (e.g., alcohol).

Jackie recognizes her need for psychological help, but little beyond that. She could be more motivated academically, but only on her own terms (which are unrealistic). She expects others to change for her, rather than a mutual relationship with others toward a common goal. She has few positive feelings about herself; often she is confused about her behavior and then becomes self-blaming. The examiner felt that her emotional traumas are so scary that she doesn't really want to explore herself or her feelings.

Emotionally, she is unable to derive satisfaction from her environment, either at home or with her peer group. At home, Jackie feels neglected and unsupported. She is angry with her father's long absences, and resentful when he returns home to dominate the family circle.

Jackie empathizes with her mother because she perceives her mother as powerless and unhappy—especially vis-a-vis her father. Jackie attempts to put psychological distance between herself and her family, yet only to defend against her anger with them. Somewhere, Jackie recalls traumatic experience(s) early in childhood which may have affected her relationship with her parents and then with peers.

At this time, Jackie wants to be independent and live on her own, get a good job working with little kids, and find some resolution in relationships with her parents. She will need substantial therapeutic support to attain these goals.

# CHAPTER 5
## PSYCHOMETRIC PROPERTIES

The relevance or irrelevance of psychometric support for projective techniques has been strenuously debated for many years (e.g., Batsche & Peterson, 1983; Gittleman, 1980; Gittleman-Klein, 1978; Knoff, 1983; Nunnally, 1978). Some assert the need to demonstrate adequate psychometric qualities before a projective technique can be effectively and appropriately used. Others consider this requirement unnecessary given the positive contribution of projective techniques and their established place in a multimethod personality assessment battery (Cascio & Sibley, 1979; Nay, 1979; Rabin & Hayes, 1978). Although obviously important, this debate falls outside the scope of this Handbook. Our own position is perhaps best summarized by Strupp and Hadley (1977) who emphasize the need for "clinical judgment, aided by behavioral observations and psychological tests of such variables as self-concept, sense of identity, balance of psychic forces, unified outlook on life, resistance to stress, self-regulation, ability to cope with reality, absence of mental and behavioral symptoms, adequacy in love, work, and play, adequacy in interpersonal relations" (p. 190).

### Kinetic Family Drawing

#### History

As noted in Chapter 1, the KFD was developed by Burns and Kaufman (1970, 1972) as a diagnostic and interpretive improvement over the *Draw-A-Family* (DAF; Hulse, 1951, 1952). Although the DAF had some exposure in the United States (Caglar, 1979–80; Deren, 1975; Gendre, Chetrit, & Dupont, 1977), it has been even more popular abroad (Cain & Gomila, 1953; Corman, 1964; Flury, 1954; Parot, 1965; Widlocher, 1965). A related technique, the *Family Drawing Scale*, has also been reported during the past few years (Bauknight, 1977; Bentley, 1979; Van Krevelen, 1975).

The KFD, nonetheless, does appear to provide more extensive, immediate, and useful data than the DAF and *Family Drawing Scale*. Burns and Kaufman (1970) noted that DAFs are generally family portraits which depict relatively static figures and often do not vary in subsequent drawings by the same child. Their comparisons of children's DAFs and KFDs strikingly emphasized the KFD's greater potential to uncover children's perceptions and attitudes toward individual and conjoint family members. Children's positive and negative relationships with family members, and their self-concepts, are more easily identified in their KFDs by their physical and psychological positions relative to other family members.

Many differences between DAFs and KFDs come from semantic and interpretive differences inherent in their directions. When asked to "Draw your family (for me)" (DAF; Hulse, 1951), many children draw individual and psychologically separate family members. There is no implicit nor explicit need for these members to be interacting (or not interacting) in a family-like way: The fact that they are drawn together on one piece of paper satisfies the directions and the definition of the group as "a family." However, when asked to "Draw a picture of everyone in your family, including you, doing something . . . some kind of action" (KFD; Burns & Kaufman, 1970), "a family" is defined as the child understands and experiences it—explicitly, as a group of interacting (or not interacting) individuals which form an interdependent unit. Certainly the gestalt principle is well applied to the family: The whole (family) is greater (more dynamic and understandable) than the sum of its parts (individual members). Finally, the KFD directions *give the child permission* to pictorially represent the past, current, or future status of the family from the child's perspective. Thus, the examiner can immediately discuss the dynamics represented in the child's KFD and explore issues the child recognizes (consciously or not) or needs to discuss. With the DAF, however, the examiner may need to ask the child to interject "action" into the picture and may be less certain of the family's interactions, individual roles, and psychological patterns.

#### Normative Studies

There have been relatively few studies providing normative data on the KFD. This may be because many find statistical comparisons unnecessary with this projective, clinically oriented technique or see little additional information forthcoming from such comparisons. Further, the lack of one demonstrated objective scoring system accepted by a majority of clinicians makes any normative study questionable in terms of generalizability.

Those normative studies that are available, however, cover a broad age range. MacNaughton (1974, cited in Burns, 1982) reported normative data based on 314 4-

and 5-year-olds. Jacobson (1973) provided normative data on public school children ages 6 through 9. Finally, Thompson (1975) reported the data from 197 suburban adolescents ages 13 through 18. All these studies involve "typical" children. Burns and Kaufman (1972) have described the KFDs of 193 clinic patients ages 5 through 20 and provided summary "norms." Meyers (1978) studied mixed samples of "typical" and clinic children and adolescents. The results of these studies are summarized below.

In a study of "typical" children, MacNaughton (1974, cited in Burns, 1982) examined the KFDs of 314 4- and 5-year-olds (51% age 4, 49% age 5; 55% boys, 45% girls). The results showed that 4-year-old girls elevated the mother figure twice as often as 5-year-old girls. For boys, however, the opposite was found: 5-year-old boys elevated the mother figure twice as often as 4-year-old boys.

Jacobson (1973) studied 136 typical public school children ages 6 through 9 years old. Analyzing the KFDs by sex and age across Burns and Kaufman's (1970, 1972) five interpretive categories, results indicated that all individual drawing characteristics and features, except for elevated figures, omission of body parts, lining at the bottom of the page, and the presence of a sun, occurred rarely or less than 16% of the time. These exceptions did not vary over age and sex. The author noted the KFD's potential utility and recommended that future research consider her study as prototypical.

Thompson (1975) studied 197 middle-class suburban adolescents ages 13 through 18 years old. The findings include the following:

1. Nearly all actions (91%) were classified as work, recreation, or personal interaction.
2. Girls ages 13 and 14 tended to draw the self figure largest most of the time.
3. Girls ages 17 and 18 tended to draw the father figure largest.
4. Adolescent figures were most often drawn in play actions and parent figures in work actions; older sisters were depicted most often as involved.
5. Male figures were often in destructive actions and mothers in constructive activity.
6. The most-used styles were encapsulation, compartmentalization, and heavy shading.
7. Males drew more expansively as age increased; constricted drawings of boys age 16 and older indicated greater likelihood of social disturbance than drawing expansively.
8. Females showed a greater degree of expansiveness at all ages.

In a study of clinically labeled or evaluated children and adolescents, Burns and Kaufman (1972) used the cumulative data of those clients assessed in their clinic settings and described in their two books (Burns & Kaufman, 1970, 1972). The 128 males ranged in age from 5 to 17 ($M = 10.14$), and the 65 females ranged in age from 5 to 20 ($M = 10.33$). Table 1 shows the most frequent actions by the father figure, mother figure, and self figure, as well as the most frequent KFD styles.

Meyers (1978) studied mixed samples of "typical" and clinically labeled or referred children. The samples included 116 boys ages 6 through 8 and 12 through 14. Of these, 60 were "typical" and 56 were emotionally disturbed (30 typical and 28 emotionally disturbed in each age group). The younger age group demonstrated fewer

**Table 1**

**Most Frequent KFD Actions and Styles in a Clinic Sample**

| Actions by Father Figure | | | | Actions by Mother Figure | | | | Actions by Self Figure | | | | Styles | |
|---|---|---|---|---|---|---|---|---|---|---|---|---|---|
| Girls ($n = 57$) | | Boys ($n = 120$) | | Girls ($n = 64$) | | Boys ($n = 124$) | | Girls ($n = 65$) | | Boys ($n = 128$) | | Total Sample ($n = 193$) | |
| Action | % | Action | % | Action | % | Action | % | Action | % | Action | % | Style | % |
| Reading | 7 | Mowing | 8 | Cooking | 14 | Cooking | 16 | Playing | 6 | Playing | 13 | Compartmentalization | 20.8 |
| Cooking | 5 | Cutting | 8 | Washing dishes | 8 | Helping | 6 | Eating | 6 | Eating | 6 | Encapsulation | 13.0 |
| Working | 5 | Reading | 6 | Making beds | 6 | Ironing | 6 | Walking | 6 | Throwing | 5 | Bottom lining | 12.0 |
| Burning | 4 | Repairing | 5 | Playing with | 5 | Planting | 5 | Riding | 5 | Riding | 5 | Underlining figures | 9.9 |
| Mowing | 4 | Painting | 5 | Vacuuming | 5 | Vacuuming | 5 | Washing dishes | 5 | Watching TV | 5 | Edging | 6.3 |
| Helping | 4 | Watching TV | 5 | | | Sweeping | 4 | | | | | Top lining | 4.2 |
| | | Working | 5 | | | Washing dishes | 4 | | | | | Folding compartmentalization | 2.1 |
| | | | | | | Sewing | 4 | | | | | | |

*Note.* Percentages represent only the most common categories and, thus, do not sum to 100%. Adapted from Burns and Kaufman (1972).

force fields, fewer arm extensions, and fewer compartmentalizations. No age differences were found for relative height of figures, barriers, physical distance between figures, erasures, description of action, body parts, rotations, bottom and top lining, encapsulation, edged placement, evasions, number of people, back placement, and underlining figures. On the adjustment variable, adjusted boys demonstrated significantly fewer instances than disturbed boys for the characteristics of barriers, physical distance, description of action, body parts, rotations, bottom and top lining, encapsulation, edged placement, evasions, and number of people.

## Reliability

Two types of reliability have been reported in the KFD literature: interrater and test-retest. Interrater reliability was examined by McPhee and Wegner (1976), who studied the drawings of emotionally disturbed children. The drawings were rated according to five stylistic categories: compartmentalization, lining at the bottom and top, underlining individual figures, edging, and folding compartmentalization. Interrater agreement among five independent judges ranged from .65 to 1.00, with a median reliability of .87. Ratings for underlining individual figures were least reliable, whereas edging and folding compartmentalization were unanimously detected because of their low incidence and easy identifiability. This study indicates high interrater reliability for the KFD, as long as the scoring criteria are clearly defined and the judges are trained adequately.

Cummings (1980) evaluated both interrater reliability and test-retest stability of the KFDs of behavior-disordered, learning-disabled, and regular-education children (*N* = 111) who were equivalent on the variables of age, sex, ethnicity, IQ, and SES (occupation of head of household). Two male and two female examiners randomly assessed the students five weeks apart. Scoring was completed using variables from three sets of objective scoring criteria (McPhee & Wegner, 1976; Meyers, 1978; O'Brien & Patton, 1974). The results indicated that all three scoring methods produced high interscorer reliabilities. The test-retest stability, however, was unstable, suggesting that certain KFD variables are sensitive to children's transitory personality states. However, this hypothesis is tentative since no measures correlating the experimental subjects' personality dimensions over the five weeks were available.

Mostkoff and Lazarus (1983) reported their own objective KFD scoring system and assessed the interrater reliabilities and test-retest reliabilities from 50 elementary school children's KFDs obtained two weeks apart. The interrater reliabilities (calculated as percentages of agreement) ranged from 86 to 100% agreement, with a mean of 97% over two raters. In each case, test-retest reliabilities were estimated across 20 separate dimensions (see "Studies of Objective Scoring Systems," p. 57). Of the 20 dimensions, nine demonstrated significant stability: self in picture, omission of body parts of other figures, arm extensions, rotated figures, elevated figures, evasions, omissions of body parts of self, barriers, and drawings on back of page. Based on these results, Mostkoff and Lazarus agreed with Cummings (1980) that KFDs appear to measure primarily state, as opposed to trait, characteristics.

## Validity

Two types of validity have been reported in the KFD literature: (a) concurrent validity, and (b) construct validity using "known groups"—a method which evaluates the KFD's ability to discriminate among children who are already clinically diagnosed or otherwise labeled.

The only concurrent validity study found in the literature (Sims, 1974) favorably correlated the KFD with the *Family Relations Indicator* (Howells & Lickorish, 1967) for 100 emotionally disturbed children in Great Britain. Given the unknown cross-cultural factors, other concurrent validity studies evaluating the KFD with established clinical scales or techniques in the United States are needed. Concurrent and other validity studies evaluating the KFD characteristics and scoring variables (e.g., Brannigan et al., 1982) are integrated into the KFD interpretations in Chapter 3.

Construct validity using the "known groups" method has been demonstrated in KFD studies with children from intact versus divorced homes (Johnston, 1975), with adolescent male delinquents (Sobel & Sobel, 1976), with siblings of severely emotionally disturbed children (Heineman, 1975; McPhee & Wegner, 1976), in the discrimination of child abuse (Schornstein & Derr, 1978), and to identify effective foster home placements (Brown, 1977).

Rhine (1978) investigated the validity of the KFD with 65 fourth and fifth graders. First, he separated the sample into high- and low-adjustment groups using the *California Test of Personality* (Thorpe, Clark, & Tiegs, 1953). Then he administered and scored the KFD using Burns and Kaufman's (1972) criteria. Nonparametric analyses revealed that there were no significant KFD differences between the high- and low-adjustment groups. While this study may cast doubt on the validity of Burns and Kaufman's assumption that KFDs correlate with general adjustment, other explanations for the results are also possible (e.g., the low-adjustment group may have been *relatively* low, not significantly low in a clinical sense; failure to control covariants such as IQ or SES; the lack of robustness with nonparametric techniques; problems with the discriminant validity of the criterion measure).

McGregor (1979) conducted a validity study involving 157 children ages 5½ to 13½ who were divided into three "treatment" groups: (a) a group of public school children rated "normal" by their teachers; (b) a conduct-problem group characterized as aggressive, acting out, and undercontrolled; and (c) a personality-problem group described as fearful, phobic, shy, and overcontrolled. McGregor compared these groups using a 3 x 2 x 2 factorial design (Problem Group x Age x Sex). He found that: (a) figure omissions (self, mother, father, sibling) were unrelated to age, sex, or problem group; (b) there was no relationship between average figure size or number of figures drawn for age group, sex, or problem group; (c) older children separated their figures significantly farther than younger children; (d) "normal" children drew their parents farther apart than either "clinical" group and were more likely to place a barrier between themselves and either parent than the conduct-problem group; (e) the conduct-problem group was more likely to place a barrier between the self and father figures than the personality-problem group; and (f) the "normal" group drew more complex drawings (more drawn figures or objects) than either of the referred groups.

McGregor concluded that the KFD is not a valid instrument for discriminating among "normal" and "clinical" children. While this may be true, the KFD and other projective tests may still serve a useful function by identifying state-oriented personality/behavioral issues that may be significant to a child (Knoff, 1983). Further, McGregor's study has several major limitations. First, the three "clinical" groupings were not based on external, verifiable criteria. Second, the study failed to covary intelligence level or socioeconomic status in the analysis. Finally, the analysis included only two age groupings despite an age range of eight years.

## Studies of Clinical Use

If surveys of psychologists using the various family drawing techniques and comparative numbers of books and journal articles are reliable and valid indices, the KFD technique is by far the most used and popular. The KFD has been used with emotionally and behaviorally disturbed children and adolescents (Burns, 1982; Burns & Kaufman, 1970, 1972; McPhee & Wegner, 1976), learning-disabled children (Raskin & Bloom, 1979), children with perceptual-motor delays (Raskin & Pitcher, 1977), black, Hispanic, and white mentally retarded children (Mangum, 1976), abused children (Schornstein & Derr, 1978), diabetic children (Sayed & Leaverton, 1974), and normative samples of children (Brewer, 1981; Jacobson, 1973) and adolescents (Thompson, 1975).

Many of the significant findings from these studies are summarized below.

Raskin and Bloom (1979) separated 50 children, referred to a psychoeducational evaluation clinic to assess suspected learning disabilities, into two age groups (ages 6 to 10 and 10½ to 16). The KFDs of these children were analyzed for feelings of isolation or rejection, bodily or somatic concerns, and sibling rivalry. The results suggest that these children did have emotional concerns (feelings of isolation, bodily concerns) regardless of their age group. The authors concluded that the KFD is useful as a clinical and research tool with learning-disabled populations.

In another study, Raskin and Pitcher (1977) compared the KFDs of average-IQ kindergarten and first-grade children with and without significant perceptual-motor delays. The two groups were matched by age ($M$ = 6.2 years) and sex (48 boys and 52 girls). Then their KFDs were evaluated for signs of isolation/rejection, bodily concerns, and sibling rivalry using Burns and Kaufman's (1970, 1972) and Koppitz' (1968) scoring criteria. Nonparametric statistics were used and indicated that children with perceptual-motor delays manifested greater isolation/rejection and bodily concerns compared to normal controls, whereas rivalry issues were equally prevalent in both samples. Raskin and Pitcher concluded that those interacting with children who have perceptual-motor delays should consider the possibility of concomitant social-emotional difficulties, and should try to integrate both educational and emotional areas in their remedial plans.

Mangum (1976) gave the *Draw-A-Person* and KFD to black, Hispanic, and white mentally retarded children ($N$ = 90) to investigate their different family identifications. The results revealed that: (a) black, Hispanic, and white children do identify with specific family members; (b) the three groups did not significantly differ in identification with specific family members; (c) the three groups did not significantly differ in their same- and cross-sex identification with specific family members; and (d) the KFD appears to be a useful technique with educable mentally retarded children ages 10 to 12.

Schornstein and Derr (1978) investigated families referred for child abuse by asking the *parents*—not the children—to produce the KFD. They found the drawings helpful in assessing family relationships, determining the parents' perspectives of their (abused) children, identifying the primary abusive parent, and evaluating the family's ecology and environment (i.e., whether the abuse was reactive or situational).

Sayed and Leaverton (1974) evaluated the KFDs of 52 diabetic children on insulin and 52 "typical" children, matching for age, sex, and ethnic characteristics. The

KFDs were evaluated for isolation and closeness of figures, aggression, presence of food and sexual themes, general body distortions, anxiety, denial of body parts, distortion of head and neck, and distortion of arms and hands. The children with diabetes showed more examples of isolation in their drawings which correlated with a number of aggression indices. The authors concluded that families with diabetic children may have unique dynamics which affect family interactions and relationships, and that the KFD may be useful in investigating these dynamics.

The KFD has also been used and investigated cross-culturally, extending its historical roots in France and Germany. To date, KFD studies have been reported in Japan (Kato, 1979; Kato, Ikura, & Kubo, 1976; Kato & Shimizu, 1978), Great Britain (Freeman, 1971), Brazil (Souza de Joode, 1976), Norway (Landmark, 1975, cited in Burns, 1982), Germany (Roth & Huber, 1979), and the Phillipines (Ledesma, 1979).

## Studies of Objective Scoring Systems

As discussed above, the development of a reliable and valid objective scoring system for the KFD would facilitate the generalizability of KFD studies as well as establish a common "language." To date, four studies using objective scoring systems have been reported in the literature.

O'Brien and Patton (1974) developed an objective scoring system through a step-wise regression analysis using 29 raw KFD scoring measures, the *Coopersmith Self-Esteem Inventory* (Coopersmith, 1959), the *Children's Manifest Anxiety Scale* (Castenada, McCandless, & Palermo, 1956), and a teacher-completed *School Behavior Checklist* (Miller, 1976) with 79 fourth- through eighth-grade public school children.

As adapted by Burns (1982), O'Brien and Patton's objective variables can be separated into Action; Figure Characteristics; and Position, Distance, and Barrier variables. Table 2 presents the quantification of these variables. Note that many categories (e.g., activity level, communication level) include variables for mother, father, and self figures. The scores corresponding to each variable are the same for the three figures, but each should be scored separately. Burns added one final variable to empirically assess whether the child would like to live in the KFD family he or she has drawn. This variable is assigned a score from 0 to 4 based on the following criteria: 0 = definitely not, 1 = probably not, 2 = neutral, 3 = probably, and 4 = definitely.

### Table 2
### Objective Scoring Criteria for KFD Variables

| Action Variables | Score | Figure Characteristics | Score | Position, Distance, and Barriers | Score |
|---|---|---|---|---|---|
| **Activity level*** | | **Arm length*** | | **Ascendance*** | |
| Laying | 0 | Arms missing | 0 | Head in bottom 1/8 | 1 |
| Sitting | 1 | 0 to 1/8 length of body | 1 | Head in bottom 1/4 | 2 |
| Standing | 2 | 1/8 to 1/4 length of body | 2 | Head in bottom 1/2 | 3 |
| Reading | 3 | 1/4 to 3/8 length of body | 3 | Head in top 1/2 | 4 |
| Riding | 4 | 3/8 to 1/2 length of body | 4 | Head in top 1/4 | 5 |
| Doing | 5 | 1/2 to 3/4 length of body | 5 | Head in top 1/8 | 6 |
| Running | 6 | Over 3/4 length of body | 6 | | |
| Throwing | 7 | | | **Number of barriers between mother and father** | |
| Hitting | 8 | **Body*** | | | |
| | | Absent | 0 | Examiner reports the number (raw score) of barriers | |
| **Communication level*** | | Head only | 1 | | |
| Sleeping | 0 | Head and neck | 2 | | |
| Watching | 1 | Head, neck, and torso | 3 | **Number of barriers between self and father** | |
| Listening | 2 | Head, neck, torso, and leg | 4 | | |
| Talking | 3 | Complete | 5 | Examiner reports the number (raw score) of barriers | |
| Playing with (person) | 4 | | | | |
| Touching (person) | 5 | **Eyes*** | | **Number of barriers between self and mother** | |
| Holding (person) | 6 | Absent | 0 | | |
| | | Eyes with no pupils | 1 | Examiner reports the number (raw score) of barriers | |
| | | Complete eyes (plus pupils) | 2 | | |

*Note.* From O'Brien and Patton (1974).

*Variables with asterisks should be scored separately for mother, father, and self figures.          *table continued on next page . . .*

**Table 2 (Continued)**
**Objective Scoring Criteria for KFD Variables**

| Action Variables | Score | Figure Characteristics | Score | Position, Distance, and Barriers | Score |
|---|---|---|---|---|---|
| **Cooperation level*** | | **Face*** | | **Figure direction*** | |
| No cooperation | 0 | Absent | 0 | Facing out of drawing | 1 |
| Working | 1 | Eyes only | 1 | Facing away from major figures | 2 |
| Helping | 2 | Eyes plus nose or mouth | 2 | Facing into drawing | 3 |
| Playing (together) | 3 | Eyes, nose, and mouth | 3 | Facing major figures | 4 |
| Working (together) | 4 | | | | |
| | | **Facial expression*** | | **Orientation between: father and mother; father and self; mother and father; mother and self; self and mother; self and father** | |
| **Masochism level*** | | Very friendly | 1 | | |
| No masochism | 0 | Friendly | 2 | | |
| Smoking | 1 | Neutral | 3 | Both facing out of drawing | 1 |
| Being hit | 2 | Unfriendly | 4 | Both facing into drawing | 2 |
| Being kicked | 4 | Very unfriendly | 5 | One facing away from other figure, one facing toward the other | 3 |
| Being cut | 5 | | | Both facing each other | 4 |
| Being burned | 6 | **Feet*** | | | |
| Being shot | 7 | Absent | 0 | | |
| Being killed | 8 | Feet on wheels (car, bike, skates) | 1 | | |
| | | 1/4 or less length of leg | 2 | | |
| **Narcissism level*** | | 1/4 to 1/2 length of leg | 3 | | |
| No narcissism | 0 | | | | |
| Dressing | 1 | **Number of siblings** | | | |
| Combing | 2 | 0 | 0 | | |
| Grooming | 3 | 1 | 1 | | |
| Drinking | 4 | 2 | 2 | | |
| Looking in mirror | 5 | 3 | 3 | | |
| | | 4 | 4 | | |
| **Nurturance level*** | | 5 | 5 | | |
| No nurturing | 0 | 6 | 6 | | |
| Planting | 1 | 7 | 7 | | |
| Helping | 2 | 8 and above | 8 | | |
| Grooming | 3 | | | | |
| Cooking | 4 | **Missing parent** | | | |
| Touching | 5 | Mother, father, or both | 1 | | |
| Holding | 6 | | | | |
| Feeding | 7 | **Figure size*** | | | |
| | | Examiner reports the height of the figure in millimeters | | | |
| **Sadism level*** | | | | | |
| No sadism | 0 | **Teeth*** | | | |
| Hitting | 1 | Absent | 0 | | |
| Fighting | 2 | Present | 1 | | |
| Hurting | 3 | | | | |
| Kicking | 4 | | | | |
| Biting | 5 | | | | |
| Burning | 6 | | | | |
| Shooting | 7 | | | | |
| Killing | 8 | | | | |
| | | | | | |
| **Tension level*** | | | | | |
| No tension | 0 | | | | |
| Slipping | 1 | | | | |
| Hanging | 2 | | | | |
| Falling | 3 | | | | |

Predictive equations were generated from the O'Brien and Patton data for the following personality variables:

1. *Manifest anxiety.* The most predictive variable was activity level of the father figure: The greater the figure's strength and action, the greater the child's anxiety.

2. *General self-concept.* The most predictive variables were activity level of the father figure and direction in which the self figure is facing: The greater the father figure's activity, the lower the self-concept score; the more the self figure faced away from other figures or into the drawing, the greater the general self-concept.

3. *School and academic self-concept.* The most predictive variable was the number of figures in the drawing or family size: The larger the family, the greater the school and academic self-concept.

4. *Social and peer self-concept.* The most predictive variables were orientation of the father toward the self figure and the direction the father figure is facing relative to all other drawn figures: The father figure facing the self figure predicted children with greater social and peer self-concept, while the father facing away predicted poor self-concept in these areas.

5. *Aggression.* The most predictive variables were the number of siblings and the relative size of child and sibling figures compared with parental figure size: The larger the number of siblings drawn and the larger the size of child and sibling figures, the greater the aggressiveness.

6. *Withdrawal.* The most predictive variable was the sex of the child making the drawing: Females were more withdrawing than males.

7. *Hostile isolation.* The most predictive variables were the grade level and sex of the child: Hostility decreased with advancing grade levels and females tended to show greater hostile behavior.

McPhee and Wegner (1976) investigated KFD styles (compartmentalization, lining on the top and bottom, underlining individual figures, edging, folding compartmentalization, and encapsulation) with 102 emotionally disturbed children and 162 children attending public schools (both samples restricted to grades 1–6). Each KFD style was objectively evaluated along a 5-point continuum (0 = complete absence of style, 1 = mildly suggests the style, 2 = moderately suggests the style, 3 = strongly suggests the style, and 4 = meets all criteria for the style). Five judges evaluated each child's KFD and an analysis of variance assessed adjustment status (emotionally disturbed vs. "normal") and sex. Results indicated no significant sex differences or interaction effects, but found a

significant KFD style difference between the two adjustment statuses. This difference, however, contradicted previous research and expectations (Burns & Kaufman, 1970, 1972); that is, drawings of adjusted children were rated higher in style (or determinants) than those of the emotionally disturbed children. McPhee and Wegner explain these results by noting the teachers' observations that the adjusted children tended to spend more time and effort drawing their KFDs than did the emotionally disturbed children, and through discussing the adjusted children's art curriculum which may have influenced specific styles.

Meyers (1978) was critical of both the O'Brien and Patton (1974) and McPhee and Wegner (1976) studies, and attempted to develop a more refined, objective system. Meyers was critical of the O'Brien and Patton study because it did not examine all the variables considered significant by Burns and Kaufman (1970, 1972) and because it excluded emotionally disturbed children. Of the McPhee and Wegner study, Meyers noted that the comparisons of the normal and emotionally disturbed samples did not control for the effects of age, intelligence, and other potential covariates.

Meyers evaluated 116 boys, ages 6 through 8 and 12 through 14, who were assessed as either well adjusted or emotionally disturbed based on behavior ratings and other empirical scales and the clinical judgments of Board-certified psychiatrists. Thus, four experimental groups participated: older and younger, adjusted and disturbed boys. Each boy's KFD was evaluated along 21 measurable KFD styles, actions, or characteristics; the data were then analyzed in a two-way analysis of variance. The 21 variables were then grouped on the basis of these results: significant adjustment main effect, significant age main effect, significant interaction (Adjustment x Age) effect, or no significant differences. One variable, folding compartmentalization, was deleted from the data analysis because it was never exhibited. The results are summarized in Table 3.

Mostkoff and Lazarus (1983) provide the fourth objective scoring approach, primarily to assess the KFD's interrater and test-retest reliabilities discussed above. Many of the scoring criteria have already been discussed. The 20 variables evaluated by these authors were:

1. Number of people in family
2. Self in picture
3. Relative size of self in relation to other figures
4. Repetition of one same symbol (as defined by Burns & Kaufman, 1972)
5. Style (compartmentalization, edging, encapsulation, folding compartmentalization, lining on the bottom, lining on the top, underlining individual figures, normal)

**Table 3**

**Grouping of 20 KFD Variables in a Two-Way Analysis of Variance**

| Adjustment Effect (Emotionally Adjusted/ Emotionally Disturbed) | Age Effect (Younger/Older) | Interaction Effect (Adjustment x Age) | No Significant Differences |
|---|---|---|---|
| Physical distance | Force fields | Safety of figures | Relative height of figures |
| Barriers | Arm extensions | Shading | Erasures |
| Description of action | Compartmentalization | | Underlining figures |
| Body parts | | | Back placement |
| Rotations | | | |
| Bottom lining | | | |
| Top lining | | | |
| Encapsulation | | | |
| Edged placement | | | |
| Evasions | | | |
| Number of figures | | | |

*Note.* Based on Meyers (1978).

6. Evasions (stick figures or all figures drawn standing)
7. One same action of an individual figure (as defined by Burns & Kaufman, 1972)
8. Repetition of one same action between two figures
9. Arm extensions (items extending from a figure's arm)
10. Elevated figures
11. Erasures of whole figures
12. Rotated figures (90-degree rotation)
13. Omission of family member
14. Omission of body parts of self drawing (head, trunk, arms, legs, neck, feet, hands, fingers, eyes, nose, or mouth)
15. Omission of body parts of other figures (head, trunk, arms, legs, neck, feet, hands, fingers, eyes, nose, or mouth)
16. Barriers (objects, walls, or lines between figures)
17. Same shortest figure
18. Same tallest figure
19. Self next to one same figure
20. Drawings on back of page

## Kinetic School Drawing

### History

The KSD was first introduced by Prout and Phillips (1974) to complement the KFD. The KSD's main purpose is to reveal the child's attitudes toward school: the child's academic and other self-perceptions related to school, the perception of his or her teacher(s), and perceptions of peers and peer relationships. Further, the originators of this technique suggest that the KSD can be used with classroom groups to obtain data on students' perceptions of teachers and classroom environments, as well as sociometric data. Either way, Prout and Phillips noted that, because the KSD is the school analogue to the KFD, the KFD's scoring and interpretation procedures could be adapted and used with the KSD.

Since its introduction, relatively few studies with the KSD have been reported. The most significant discussion is in a monograph by Sarbaugh (1982). Although she calls her technique the *Kinetic Drawing-School* (KD-S) technique, there is little to distinguish it—either in administration or rationale—from the KSD. Sarbaugh reviews her work with the school technique including Symbolism and Levels of Interpretation, General Types and Features of the School Drawing, Features Common to Drawing-Oriented Projective Techniques, Features Specific to School Drawings, Cross-Checking Interpretational Features, and Humor and Hostility in School Drawings. Many of Sarbaugh's interpretative criteria are based on the KFD analysis (Burns & Kaufman, 1970, 1972) as well as more generic interpretations of projective figure drawings (e.g., Buck, 1964; Hammer, 1971). Interpretations specific to school drawings that are discussed by Sarbaugh (1982) are reviewed in Chapter 3.

It should be noted that, as with the KFD, some nonkinetic school drawings do exist. The interested reader is referred to Rogers and Wright (1971) and Kutnick (1978).

## Normative Studies

Sarbaugh (1982), generalizing her extensive experience with projective and kinetic drawings, has studied children and adolescents from kindergarten through high school and reported the following findings.

*Kindergarten*: Early in the year, many of these children have difficulty putting all the members of their family or class into one picture. Visual-motor coordination is a definite confounding variable with drawing skill and quality at this age. Many will draw a simplified drawing and "embellish" it through verbal description.

*Grade 1*: Inclusion of desks and other physical properties is more common.

*Grade 2*: There is a greater emphasis on buildings, rooms, and objects; people may be greatly deemphasized.

*Grade 3*: These children usually make appropriate use of props and equipment.

*Grade 4*: Fourth graders draw very complete pictures, and also may use very individualized or idiosyncratic styles in their drawings. Linear perspective may become more evident (especially if taught in art class).

*Grade 5*: Here, children usually have the visual-motor ability to draw what they want to draw (good detail, differentiation of figures and activities). Humor in drawings may become evident.

*Junior/middle/high school*: Stick figures are very commonly drawn here. Students are very open about their attitudes toward school, teachers, and peers. Drawing tends to be more rapid with shortcuts used to complete the task.

*General*: Objects such as clocks, flags, public address systems, chalkboards, and alphabet or handwriting models are commonly found in classrooms. Their presence—unless emphasized through line quality/characteristics or perseveration—often have minimal symbolic meaning.

Prout and Celmer (1984) studied 100 fifth-grade students (44 boys, 56 girls) enrolled in a regular education program. Means and standard deviations were obtained for five drawing characteristics. The mean height of the teacher figure was 54.25 mm ($SD$ = 25.25 mm) and the mean height of the self figure was 49.25 mm ($SD$ = 21.25 mm). For number of peers, the mean was 1.56 ($SD$ = 1.00). For the distances between the self and teacher figures and the self and other figures, the means were 90.00 mm ($SD$ = 79.50) and 50.25 mm ($SD$ = 70.80), respectively.

## Validity

Walton (1983) has reported two preliminary KSD studies: one study comparing Hispanic/Portuguese and Anglo children, and one study with children referred for psychological testing. In the first study comparing Hispanic and Anglo children, seven objectively scored KSD characteristics were evaluated: location of drawings (center vs. off-center placement), size deviations of drawings (regular vs. large or small size), line quality (regular vs. light or dark lines, and continuous vs. broken/sketchy lines), drawing style (presence of transparencies, erasures, overwork, shading, overly detailed work, or overly simplistic work), inclusion of people in the drawing (present or absent), and presence of conflictual scenes (yes or no). None of the comparisons reached significance, indicating that, at best, the KSD may be a relatively culturally unbiased technique with Hispanics for whom emotional disturbance placement decisions are being considered. At worst, it appears that some KSD style and content characteristics have equal probabilities of occurring on Hispanic or Anglo children's drawings.

In her second study with referred children, Walton used the same seven characteristics to evaluate the KSDs of children with intellectual limitations, learning disabilities, emotional interferences with learning, or some combination of these problems. Although admirable in its scope, results from this study are difficult to interpret. Classifications of the children were not based on objective criteria, significant correlates (e.g., IQ and age) were uncontrolled, and there were other problems in the sampling methodology which limit the generalizability of the results.

Prout and Celmer (1984) investigated the use of the KSD to predict academic achievement with 100 regular fifth-grade students. Each child's *Science Research Associates Achievement Test* (SRA; Science Research Associates, 1978) score was correlated with numerous KSD variables: self drawing placed in or out of school, self drawing engaged in undesirable behavior (e.g., yelling, fighting), self drawing engaged in academic behavior, teacher height, child height, number of peers, distance between self and teacher, distance between self and others, quantified Koppitz (1968) score for the self drawing, and quantified Reynolds (1978) score adapting his KFD guidelines to the KSD.

Point biserial (for dichotomous variables) and Pearson product-moment correlations (for continuous variables) and a stepwise multiple regression procedure were used to analyze the data. Overall, the KSD variables yielded significant multiple correlations with achievement. Of the 10 KSD variables, six correlated significantly with academic achievement and three others approached significance. Three of these six significant correlations involved negative relationships: number of peers, Reynolds score, and self drawing engaged in undesirable behavior (i.e., the less the figure was engaged in undesirable behavior, the higher the academic achievement). The other three significant correlations involved positive relationships: child height, teacher height, and self drawing engaged in academic behavior (i.e., the drawings with figures active in academic behavior predicted the higher achieving students). Prout and Celmer concluded that the KSD does have clinical value and utility, and can help to investigate perceptions/feelings toward school and their association with academic achievement. Means and standard deviations from this study are reported in the "Normative Studies" section above (see p. 61).

Schneider (1978) evaluated all elementary school students referred to a school psychologist in one academic year with the KFD and KSD to assess the validity of the KSD. Using ratings of the severity of the children's school problems and the severity of each family's problems as the dependent measures, both the KFD and KSD were included in the stepwise regression equation. However, neither added significantly to the prediction achieved by age and IQ alone. Schneider concluded that his study offered little validation support for the KSD, although it did not necessarily invalidate it as a clinically useful tool.

The limited number of KSD studies available indicates the need for further research to assess the psychometric properties of the KSD. Given its development as an analogue to the KFD, one might accept those psychometric studies with the KFD as generalizable to the KSD. This, however, should not preempt further detailed psychometric study of the KSD.

# REFERENCES

Batsche, G.M., & Peterson, D.W. (1983). School psychology and projective assessment: A growing incompatability. *School Psychology Review, 12*, 440–445.

Bauknight, C.R. (1977). Parent-child interaction in the Family Drawing Test as an indication of withdrawn behavior in children. *Dissertation Abstracts International, 38*, 1882A. (University Microfilms No. 77–22,716)

Beery, K.E. (1982). *Revised administration, scoring, and teaching manual for the Developmental Test of Visual-Motor Integration*. Cleveland: Modern Curriculum Press.

Bender, L. (1946). *Bender Visual-Motor Gestalt Test*. New York: American Orthopsychiatric Association.

Bentley, D.S. (1979). Family Drawing Scale: Relationships with intelligence, cognitive styles, sex, age, ethnic group, family size. *Dissertation Abstracts International, 39*, 5510B–5511B. (University Microfilms No. 7909511)

Brannigan, G.G., Schofield, J.J., & Holtz, R. (1982). Family drawings as measures of interpersonal distance. *The Journal of Social Psychology, 117*, 155–156.

Brewer, F.L. (1981). Children's interaction patterns in Kinetic Family Drawings. *Dissertations Abstracts International, 41*, 4253B. (University Microfilms No. 8109275)

Brown, T.R. (1977). *KFD in evaluating foster home care*. Olympia, WA: Office of Research, State of Washington, Department of Social and Health Services.

Buck, J.N. (1948). The H-T-P technique: A qualitative and quantitative scoring manual. *Journal of Clinical Psychology, 4*, 317–396.

Buck, J.N. (1964). *The House-Tree-Person (H-T-P) manual supplement*. Los Angeles: Western Psychological Services.

Buck, J.N., & Hammer, E.F. (Eds.) (1969). *Advances in House-Tree-Person technique: Variations and applications*. Los Angeles: Western Psychological Services.

Burns, R.C. (1982). *Self-growth in families: Kinetic Family Drawings (K-F-D) research and applications*. New York: Brunner/Mazel.

Burns, R.C., & Kaufman, S.F. (1970). *Kinetic Family Drawings (K-F-D): An introduction to understanding children through kinetic drawings*. New York: Brunner/Mazel.

Burns, R.C., & Kaufman, S.F. (1972). *Actions, styles, and symbols in Kinetic Family Drawings (K-F-D): An interpretive manual*. New York: Brunner/Mazel.

Cagler, H. (1979–80). Etude a travers le test du dessin de la famille des troubles des apprentissages scolaires lies a des difficultes d'identification [Use of the Draw-a-Family Test in the study of learning difficulties linked to difficulties of identification]. *Bulletin de Psychologie, 33*, 165–171.

Cain, J., & Gomila, J. (1953). Le dessin de la famille chez l'enfant, Criteres de classification [The family drawing of the child: Criteria for classification]. *Annales Medique Psychologie, 4*, 502–506.

Cascio, W.F., & Silbey, V. (1979). Utility of the assessment center as a selection device. *Journal of Applied Psychology, 64*, 107–118.

Castenada, A., McCandless, B.R., & Palermo, D.S. (1956). A children's form of the Manifest Anxiety Scale. *Child Development, 27*, 317–326.

Corman, L. (1964). *Le test du dessin de familles* [The family drawing test]. Paris: Presses de Universitaires de France.

Coopersmith, S. (1959). A method for determining types of self-esteem. *Journal of Abnormal and Social Psychology, 59*, 87–94.

Cummings, J.A. (1980). An evaluation of an objective scoring system for KFDs. *Dissertation Abstracts International, 41*, 2313B. (University Microfilms No. 8029117)

Deren, S. (1975). An empirical evaluation of the validity of a Draw-a-Family test. *Journal of Clinical Psychology, 31*, 542–546.

Fein, L.G. (1979). Current status of psychological diagnostic testing in university training programs and in delivery of service systems. *Psychological Reports, 44*, 863–879.

Flury, M. (1954). Zeichne deine familie [Draw your family]. *Praxis der Kinderpsychologie und Kinderpsychiatrie, 3*, 117–125.

Freeman, H. (1971). What child's drawings can reveal. *Mother, 35*, 34–36.

Gendre, F., Chetrit, S., & Dupont, J.B. (1977). Use of the Draw-a-Family Test with children: A preliminary study. *Revue de Psychologie Appliquee, 27*, 243–284.

Gittleman, R. (1980). The role of psychological tests for differential diagnosis in child psychiatry. *Journal of the American Academy of Child Psychiatry, 19*, 413–438.

Gittleman-Klein, R. (1978). Validity of projective tests for psychodiagnosis in children. In R.L. Spitzer & D.F. Klein (Eds.), *Critical issues in psychiatric diagnosis* (pp. 141–166). New York: Raven Press.

Goh, D.S., Teslow, C.J., & Fuller, G.B. (1981). The practice of psychological assessment among school psychologists. *Professional Psychology, 12*, 696–706.

Goodenough, F.L. (1926). *Measurement of intelligence by drawings*. New York: Harcourt, Brace, & World.

Hammer, E.F. (1971). *The clinical application of projective drawings*. Springfield, IL: C.C. Thomas.

Harris, D.B. (1963). *Children's drawings as measures of intellectual maturity*. New York: Harcourt, Brace, & World.

Harris, D.B., & Roberts, J. (1972). *Intellectual maturity of children: Demographic and sociometric factors* (DHEW, Vital and Health Statistics, Series 11, No. 116). Washington, DC: U.S. Government Printing Office.

Heineman, T. (1975). Kinetic Family Drawings of siblings of severely emotionally disturbed children. *Thesis Abstracts*, School of Social Welfare, University of California at Berkeley.

Howells, J.G., & Lickorish, J.R. (1967). *Family Relations Indicator*. Edinburgh: Oliver and Boyd.

Hulse, W.C. (1951). The emotionally disturbed child draws his family. *Quarterly Journal of Child Behavior*, *3*, 152–174.

Hulse, W.C. (1952). Childhood conflict expressed through family drawings. *Journal of Projective Techniques*, *16*, 66–79.

Jacobson, D.A. (1973). A study of Kinetic Family Drawings of public school ages 6–9. *Dissertation Abstracts International*, *34*, 2935B. (University Microfilms No. 73–29,455)

Johnston, D.D. (1975). Comparison of DAF and K-F-D in children from intact and divorced homes. *Thesis Abstracts*, California State University, San Jose.

Kato, T. (1979). *Pictorial expression of family relationships in young children*. Ninth International Congress of Psychotherapy of Expression, Verona, Italy.

Kato, T., Ikura, H., & Kubo, Y. (1976). A study on the "style" in Kinetic Family Drawing. *Japanese Bulletin of Art Therapy*, *7*, 19–25.

Kato, T., & Shimuzu, T. (1978). The action of K-F-D and the child's attitude towards family members. *Japanese Bulletin of Art Therapy*, *9*, 25–31.

Klepsch, M., & Logie, L. (1982). *Children draw and tell*. New York: Brunner/Mazel.

Knoff, H.M. (1983). Justifying projective/personality assessment in school psychology: A response to Batsche and Peterson. *School Psychology Review*, *12*, 446–451.

Koppitz, E.M. (1968). *Psychological evaluation of children's human figure drawing*. New York: Grune and Stratton.

Kutnick, P. (1978). Children's drawings of their classrooms: Development and social maturity. *Child Study Journal*, *8*, 175–185.

Ledesma, L.K. (1979). The Kinetic Family Drawings of Filipo adolescents. *Dissertation Abstracts International*, *40*, 1866B. (University Microfilms No. 7922072)

Machover, K. (1949). *Personality projection in the drawing of the human figure*. Springfield, IL: C.C. Thomas.

Mangum, M.E. (1976). Familial identification in Black, Anglo, and Chicano MR children using K-F-D. *Dissertation Abstracts International*, *36*, 7343A. (University Microfilms No. 76–10,846)

McGregor, J.P. (1979). Kinetic Family Drawing Test: A validity study. *Dissertation Abstracts International*, *40*, 927B–928B. (University Microfilms No. 7918101)

McPhee, I.P., & Wegner, K.W. (1976). Kinetic Family Drawing styles and emotionally disturbed childhood behavior. *Journal of Personality Assessment*, *40*, 487–491.

Meyers, D. (1978). Toward an objective evaluation procedure for the Kinetic Family Drawings (KFD). *Journal of Personality Assessment*, *42*, 358–365.

Miller, L.C. (1976). *School Behavior Checklist*. Los Angeles: Western Psychological Services.

Mostkoff, D.L., & Lazarus, P.J. (1983). The Kinetic Family Drawing: The reliability of an objective scoring system. *Psychology in the Schools*, *20*, 16–20.

Nay, W.R. (1979). *Multimethod clinical assessment*. New York: Gardner.

Nunnally, J.C. (1978). An overview of psychological measurement. In B.B. Wolman (Ed.), *Clinical diagnosis of mental disorders: A handbook* (pp. 97–146). New York: Plenum Press.

O'Brien, R.O., & Patton, W.F. (1974). Development of an objective scoring method for the Kinetic Family Drawing. *Journal of Personality Assessment*, *38*, 156–164.

Ogdon, D.P. (1977). *Psychodiagnostics and personality assessment: A handbook* (2nd ed.). Los Angeles: Western Psychological Services.

Ogdon, D.P. (1982). *Handbook of psychological signs, symptoms, and syndromes*. Los Angeles: Western Psychological Services.

Parot, M. (1965). Le dessin de la famille [The family drawing]. *Revue de Psychologie Applique*, *15*, 179–192.

Prout, H.T. (1983). School psychologists and social-emotional assessment techniques: Patterns in training and use. *School Psychology Review*, *12*, 377–383.

Prout, H.T., & Celmer, D.S (1984). School drawings and academic achievement: A validity study of the Kinetic School Drawing technique. *Psychology in the Schools*, *21*, 176–180.

Prout, H.T., & Phillips, P.D. (1974). A clinical note: The Kinetic School Drawing. *Psychology in the Schools*, *11*, 303–306.

Rabin, A.I., & Hayes, D.L. (1978). Concerning the rationale of diagnostic testing. In B.B. Wolman (Ed.), *Clinical diagnosis of mental disorders: A handbook* (pp. 579–600). New York: Plenum Press.

Raskin, L.M., & Bloom, A.S. (1979). Kinetic Family Drawings by children with learning disabilities. *Journal of Pediatric Psychology*, *4*, 247–251.

Raskin, L.M., & Pitcher, G.B. (1977). Kinetic Family Drawings by children with perceptual-motor delays. *Journal of Learning Disabilities*, *10*, 370–374.

Reynolds, C.R. (1978). A quick-scoring guide to the interpretation of children's Kinetic Family Drawings (KFD). *Psychology in the Schools*, *15*, 489–492.

Rhine, P.C. (1978). Adjustment indicators in Kinetic Family Drawings by children: A validation study. *Dissertation Abstracts International*, *39*, 995B. (University Microfilms No. 7813108)

Rogers, R., & Wright, E. (1971). A study of children's drawings of the classrooms. *Journal of Educational Research*, *64*, 370–374.

Roth, J.W., & Huber, B.L. (1979). Kinetic Family Drawings. *Familien Dynamik*, Sonderdruck. Stuttgart: Klett-Cotta.

Sarbaugh, M.E.A. (1982). Kinetic Drawing-School (KD-S) Technique. *Illinois School Psychologists' Association Monograph Series, 1,* 1–70.

Sayed, A.J., & Leaverton, D.R. (1974). Kinetic Family Drawings of children with diabetes. *Child Psychiatry and Human Development, 5,* 40–50.

Schneider, G.B. (1978). A preliminary validation study of the Kinetic School Drawing. *Dissertation Abstracts International, 38,* 6628A. (University Microfilms No. 7805520)

Schornstein, H.M., & Derr, J. (1978). The many applications of Kinetic Family Drawings in child abuse. *British Journal of Projective Psychology and Personality Study, 23,* 33–35.

Science Research Associates. (1978). *Science Research Associates Achievement Test.* Chicago: Author.

Sims, C.A. (1974). Kinetic Family Drawings and the Family Relations Indicator. *Journal of Clinical Psychology, 30,* 87–88.

Sobel, M., & Sobel, W. (1976). Discriminating adolescent male delinquents through the use of Kinetic Family Drawings. *Journal of Personality Assessment, 40,* 91–94.

Souza de Joode, M. (1976). O desenho cinetico da familia (KFD) como instrumento de diagnostico da dinamica do relacionamento familiar [The Kinetic Family Drawing (KFD) as a diagnostic instrument for family dynamics and relationships]. *Auquivos Brasileiros de Psicologia Aplicada, 29,* 149–162.

Strupp, H.H., & Hadley, S.W. (1977). A tripartite model of mental health and therapeutic outcomes. *American Psychologist, 32,* 187–196.

Thompson, L.V. (1975). Kinetic Family Drawings of adolescents. *Dissertation Abstracts International, 36,* 3077B–3078B. (University Microfilms No. 75-29,095)

Thorpe, L.P., Clark, W.W., & Tiegs, E.W. (1953). *California Test of Personality.* Monterey, CA: McGraw-Hill.

Van Krevelen, D.A. (1975). On the use of a Family Drawing Test. *Acta Paedopsychiatrica, 41,* 104–109.

Wade, T.C., Baker, T.B., Morton, T.L., & Baker, L.J. (1978). The status of psychological testing in clinical psychology: Relationships between test use and professional activities and orientation. *Journal of Personality Assessment, 42,* 3–10.

Wagner, E.E. (1983). *The Hand Test revised manual.* Los Angeles: Western Psychological Services.

Walton, J.R. (1983, March). *Kinetic School Drawings of referred school children.* Paper presented at the National Association of School Psychologists, Detroit.

Widlocher, D. (1965). *L'interpretation des dessins d'enfants* [The interpretation of children's drawings]. Brussels: Charles Dessart.

Zuk, G.H. (1978). Values and family therapy. *Psychotherapy: Theory, Research and Practice, 15,* 48–55.

# Kinetic Drawing System for Family and School
## Scoring Booklet
Howard M. Knoff, Ph.D.

*Published by*
**WESTERN PSYCHOLOGICAL SERVICES**

**WPS**® 12031 Wilshire Boulevard
Los Angeles, CA 90025-1251
— *Publishers and Distributors* —

Child's Name: _____ Sex: M  F

Address: _____ Phone: _____

Ethnic Background: _____ Grade: _____ Date Tested: _____
year   month   day

School Name: _____ Birthdate: _____
year   month   day

Teacher Name: _____ Age at Time of Testing: _____
year   month   day

Referred by: _____ Examiner Name: _____

Reason for Referral: _____

Qualitative Administrative Observations: _____

_____

_____

_____

Case History and Diagnostic Data: _____

_____

_____

_____

## ADMINISTRATION DIRECTIONS

It is recommended that the *Kinetic Family Drawing* (KFD) be given first, followed by the *Kinetic School Drawing* (KSD). Give the child a #2 pencil with eraser and a sheet of plain white 8½″ x 11″ paper. Then, for the KFD, say:

**"Draw a picture of everyone in your family, including you, DOING something. Try to draw whole people, not cartoons or stick people. Remember, make everyone DOING something—some kind of action."**

There is no time limit for the drawing. After the child has completed the drawing, take away the pencil and administer the inquiry phase (see last page of this booklet for suggested questions).

Immediately after completing the inquiry phase for the KFD, administer the KSD. Give the child the pencil and a second, clean sheet of paper. Say:

**"I'd like you to draw a school picture. Put yourself, your teacher, and a friend or two in the picture. Make everyone doing something. Try to draw whole people and make the best drawing you can. Remember, draw yourself, your teacher, and a friend or two, and make everyone doing something."**

Again, there is no time limit. When the child has completed the drawing, take the pencil away and give the inquiry phase for the KSD.

## SCORING DIRECTIONS

Check all characteristics below that are evident in the child's drawings. First, place a checkmark or "X" in the KFD column for each characteristic evident in the child's KFD. Then place a checkmark or "X" in the KSD column for each characteristic evident in the child's KSD. Note that the KSD includes most of the characteristics assessed in the KFD as well as some additional characteristics specific to the school setting. In the space provided on the right, list any specific details regarding the drawings. See the Interpretation chapter of the Handbook for information to assist in determining the most appropriate hypotheses for each characteristic.

| KFD | KSD | CHARACTERISTICS | NOTES |
|-----|-----|-----------------|-------|
| | | **Actions of and Between Figures** | |
| ☐ | ☐ | Ball (e.g., baseballs/footballs being thrown between figures) | |
| ☐ | ☐ | Large ball | |
| ☐ | ☐ | Ball directed towards a specific figure | |
| ☐ | ☐ | Ball directed away from figure, or being held, or aloft in no particular direction | |
| ☐ | ☐ | Self not playing | |
| ☐ | ☐ | Ball-playing isolated to one figure | |
| ☐ | ☐ | Ball-bouncing with self or isolated to one figure | |
| ☐ | ☐ | Ball on the head | |
| ☐ | ☐ | Numerous balls on the head | |
| ☐ | | Entire family playing ball together | |
| ☐ | ☐ | Hanging or falling figures (e.g., drawing of individuals in precarious positions) | |
| ☐ | ☐ | Dirt themes (e.g., getting dirty, digging in dirt) | |
| ☐ | ☐ | Skin diving | |
| | | Mother actions | |
| ☐ | | Cooking | |
| ☐ | | Cleaning | |
| ☐ | | Ironing | |
| | | Father actions | |
| ☐ | | Household activities | |
| ☐ | | Driving to or at work | |
| ☐ | | Cutting | |
| ☐ | | High activity level (e.g., running, throwing, cutting, hitting) | |
| ☐ | | Father figure facing the self figure | |
| ☐ | ☐ | Position of figures with respect to safety (e.g., figure in dangerous position [through visible or verbal description]) | |
| | ☐ | Self figure engaged in academic behavior (e.g., figure engaged in reading, calculating, giving an answer appropriately) | |
| | ☐ | Self figure engaged in undesirable behavior (e.g., figure inappropriately engaged in yelling, fighting, running) | |
| | ☐ | Recess activity/actions (or other nonacademic activities—lunch, music, gym) | |
| | | **Figure Characteristics** | |
| | | *Individual Figure Characteristics* | |
| ☐ | ☐ | "Picasso" eye (single eye drawn disoriented on or in the middle of a figure's face) | |
| ☐ | ☐ | Jagged or sharp finger, toes, teeth | |
| | | Long or extended arm | |
| ☐ | ☐ | In other than self drawing | |
| ☐ | ☐ | In self drawing | |
| ☐ | ☐ | Between two figures | |

| KFD | KSD | CHARACTERISTICS | NOTES |
|---|---|---|---|
| ☐ | ☐ | Shading or cross-hatching (scribbling or "blacking out" of a figure, or heavy shading [all except hair]) | |
| ☐ | ☐ | Blackening of specific body part | |
| ☐ | ☐ | General blackening | |
| ☐ | ☐ | Blackening an individual or object | |
| ☐ | ☐ | Body part "cut off" or occluded by another object | |
| ☐ | ☐ | Cutting off the head | |
| ☐ | | Presence of barriers between self and mother figure | |
| ☐ | ☐ | Omission of body parts | |
| ☐ | ☐ | Omission of feet | |
| ☐ | ☐ | Omission of face in self drawing | |
| ☐ | ☐ | Transparencies (visible internal organs) | |
| ☐ | ☐ | Drawing idealized picture of oneself (determined primarily through inquiry process) | |
| | | *Global/Comparative Figure Characteristics* | |
| | | Number of figures in the drawing | |
| ☐ | | Large family (in absolute numbers) | |
| ☐ | | Large or greater number of siblings drawn | |
| | ☐ | Large number of peers drawn (significantly greater than 2) | |
| | ☐ | Lack of people drawn (or people represented symbolically by other objects) | |
| | | Relative height of figures | |
| ☐ | ☐ | Small self drawing (relative to other figures in the drawing) | |
| ☐ | ☐ | Large drawings (relative to other figures in the drawing) | |
| ☐ | | Self and sibling figures drawn relatively larger than parents | |
| ☐ | ☐ | Self drawing largest | |
| ☐ | | Mother figure largest | |
| ☐ | | Father figure largest | |
| | ☐ | Large self or child drawing (significantly greater than 49.25 mm) | |
| | ☐ | Large teacher relative to self drawing | |
| | ☐ | Large teacher drawing (significantly greater than 55 mm) | |
| ☐ | ☐ | Similar treatment of figures | |
| ☐ | ☐ | Differential treatment of figures | |
| ☐ | ☐ | Elevated self drawing | |
| ☐ | ☐ | Elevated drawing of significant other | |
| ☐ | ☐ | Self figure facing away from other figures or facing into the drawing | |
| ☐ | ☐ | Crossing out and redrawing of an entire figure | |
| | | Omission of figures | |
| ☐ | ☐ | Omission of others (failure to draw a significant other such as mother, father, sibling, teacher) | |
| ☐ | ☐ | Omission of self | |
| ☐ | ☐ | Inclusion of extra figures | |
| ☐ | ☐ | Stick figures (where *all* figures are drawn as stick figures) | |
| ☐ | ☐ | Evasions (one or more, but not all, drawings depicting stick figures or no action) | |
| ☐ | ☐ | Bizarre figures (e.g., robots, animalistic features) | |
| | ☐ | Characteristics of teacher drawing | |
| | ☐ | Excessively detailed teacher drawing | |

**Position, Distance, and Barriers**

*Position Characteristics*

Placement of figures on the page

| KFD | KSD | |
|-----|-----|---|
| ☐ | ☐ | Drawing self next to significant other |
| ☐ | ☐ | Drawing self significantly apart from others who are grouped in the picture |
| ☐ | | Drawing of self between parents |
| ☐ | ☐ | Lack of interaction/integration of figures (no figure facing another, figures with backs or sides to each other, figures doing separate/individual activities or actions) |
| ☐ | | Parental figures individually not interacting with other figures |
| ☐ | ☐ | Rotated figures (rotation of self figure) |
| ☐ | ☐ | Ordering of figures |
| ☐ | | All family members in chronological order with figure size corresponding to each member's respective age |

*Distance Characteristics*

Physical distance between figures (distance between self drawing and mother figure, father figure, or other authority figure)

| KFD | KSD | |
|-----|-----|---|
| ☐ | ☐ | General |
| ☐ | ☐ | Close |
| ☐ | ☐ | Distant |

*Barriers*

| KFD | KSD | |
|-----|-----|---|
| ☐ | ☐ | Fields of force (a force or action between figures, such as throwing a ball, knife, airplane, etc.) |
| ☐ | ☐ | The "A" syndrome or phenomenon (the presence of objects in a drawing where an "A" is embedded prominently [through shading or line reinforcement] in the object, and where the object is pictorially related to someone in the drawing) |
| ☐ | ☐ | The "X" syndrome or phenomenon (the presence of objects in a drawing where an "X" is embedded prominently [through shading or line reinforcement] in the object, and where the object is pictorially related to someone in the drawing) |
| ☐ | | "X" present in the legs supporting an ironing board |

**Style**

Line quality

| KFD | KSD | |
|-----|-----|---|
| ☐ | ☐ | Light, broken, or uneven |
| ☐ | ☐ | Heavy, overworked |
| ☐ | ☐ | Unsteady, wavy |
| ☐ | ☐ | Asymmetric drawing |
| ☐ | ☐ | Excessive attention to details |
| ☐ | ☐ | Transparencies |
| ☐ | ☐ | Erasures |
| ☐ | ☐ | Compartmentalization (characterized by the intentional separation of individuals in a drawing by using one or more [straight] lines) |
| ☐ | ☐ | Compartmentalizing a significant other |
| ☐ | ☐ | Compartmentalizing all figures (all performing separate activities) |
| ☐ | ☐ | Compartmentalizing two or more figures together |
| ☐ | ☐ | Encapsulation (exists when one or more figures [but not all] are enclosed by an object's encircling lines [e.g., a jump rope, airplane, car] and/or by lines which do not stretch the length of the page) |
| ☐ | ☐ | Encapsulating two figures together |
| ☐ | ☐ | Folding compartmentalization (folding the paper into discrete sections or boundaries) |
| ☐ | ☐ | Lining at the top (lines drawn along the *entire* top of a drawing or above specific drawn individuals where *more than one line* extends across the drawing) |

| KFD | KSD | CHARACTERISTICS | NOTES |
|---|---|---|---|
| ☐ | ☐ | Underlining at the bottom of the page (occurs when *more than one line* covers the entire bottom of a drawing) | |
| ☐ | ☐ |     Lining and cross-hatching at the bottom of a page | |
| ☐ | ☐ | Underlining of individual figures (occurs when at least two lines or repetitions appear under a figure or whole person) | |
| ☐ | ☐ | Edging (style characterized by having *all* figures drawn on two or more edges of the paper [e.g., vertically, upside-down]) | |
| ☐ | ☐ | Anchoring (drawing all figures within one inch of a single edge of the paper) | |
| ☐ | ☐ | Figures drawn on the back/other side of the paper | |
| ☐ | ☐ |     Self drawing on other side of paper | |
| ☐ | ☐ | Rejecting a started drawing and redrawing an entire picture | |
| ☐ | ☐ | Perseveration or repetition of objects drawn in a picture | |
| | ☐ | Emphasis on physical features of a room (e.g., emphasis on the building, classroom walls, furniture) | |
| | | Drawing viewpoints or perspectives | |
| | ☐ |     Back views of people | |
| | ☐ |     Bird's-eye view of classroom/drawing (KSD drawn so that one seems to be looking at the drawing as if far above, as if a bird flying over the classroom) | |
| | ☐ | Outdoor pictures | |
| | | **Symbols** | |
| | ☐ | Apples | |
| ☐ | ☐ | Balloons | |
| ☐ | | Beds | |
| ☐ | |     All figures in bed(s) | |
| ☐ | ☐ | Bicycles | |
| ☐ | ☐ | Brooms | |
| ☐ | ☐ | Butterflies | |
| ☐ | ☐ | Buttons (oversized or elaborated) | |
| ☐ | ☐ | Cats | |
| | ☐ | Chalkboard or bulletin board | |
| ☐ | ☐ | Circles (preoccupation with circular drawings or objects) | |
| | ☐ | Clock | |
| ☐ | ☐ | Clowns | |
| ☐ | | Cribs | |
| ☐ | |     Heavy markings on a drawn crib | |
| ☐ | |     Repetition of crib drawing in a single picture | |
| ☐ | ☐ | Dangerous objects (prevalence of dangerous objects) | |
| ☐ | ☐ | Drums | |
| ☐ | ☐ | Flowers | |
| ☐ | ☐ |     Flowers drawn below the waist | |
| ☐ | ☐ | Garbage | |
| ☐ | ☐ |     Figures taking out the garbage | |
| ☐ | ☐ | Heat (e.g., suns, fires), light (e.g., light bulbs, lamps, floodlights), warmth (e.g., ironing, sunshine) objects/depictions in drawings | |
| ☐ | ☐ |     Hanging lights on suspended chains | |
| ☐ | ☐ |     Fire theme | |
| ☐ | ☐ |     Electricity | |
| ☐ | ☐ |     Lamp | |
| ☐ | ☐ |     Light bulbs | |

| KFD | KSD | CHARACTERISTICS | NOTES |
|:---:|:---:|---|---|
| ☐ | ☐ | Horses | |
| | | Jump rope | |
| ☐ | ☐ |    Self figure jumping rope | |
| ☐ | ☐ |    Figure (other than self) jumping rope | |
| ☐ | ☐ | Kites | |
| ☐ | ☐ | Ladders | |
| ☐ | | Lawnmowers (also hatchets, axes, sharp instruments) | |
| ☐ | |    Associated with self figure | |
| ☐ | |    Associated with other figure | |
| ☐ | ☐ | Leaves | |
| ☐ | ☐ |    Collecting leaves | |
| ☐ | |    Burning leaves | |
| ☐ | ☐ | Logs | |
| ☐ | ☐ | Moon | |
| ☐ | ☐ | Motorcycles | |
| ☐ | ☐ | Paintbrush | |
| | ☐ | Principal | |
| ☐ | ☐ | Rain | |
| ☐ | ☐ | Refrigerators | |
| | ☐ | School bus | |
| ☐ | ☐ | Snakes | |
| ☐ | ☐ | Snow (and other "cold" symbols) | |
| ☐ | ☐ | Stars | |
| ☐ | ☐ | Stop signs (also "Keep Out" signs) | |
| ☐ | ☐ | Stoves | |
| ☐ | ☐ | Sun | |
| ☐ | ☐ |    Darkened sun | |
| ☐ | ☐ |    Figures leaning toward the sun | |
| ☐ | ☐ |    Figures drawn far away from the sun, leaning away from it, or faced away from it | |
| ☐ | ☐ | Trains | |
| ☐ | ☐ | Vacuum cleaners | |
| ☐ | ☐ | Water themes (formation of water-related objects) | |
| ☐ | ☐ |    Figure floating in water | |

## The Kinetic Drawing System Inquiry Process

The inquiry phase occurs after the child has completed the KFD or KSD and after you have taken the child's pencil away. The inquiry process attempts to clarify the child's drawing and investigate the overt and covert processes which affected its production. The inquiry questions below are *suggested* questions which can be asked for each drawing and can be adapted and extended as the situation dictates. The questions may be asked in any order, and may be expanded to comprise part of a psychological interview.

1. For each figure in the drawing, ask the child that person's name, relationship to the child, age, and other meaningful characteristics or data.

2. Questions about the figures in the drawing include:
   "What is this person doing?"
   "What is good about this person?"
   "What is bad about this person?"
   "What does this person wish for?"
   "What is this person thinking?"
   "What is this person feeling?"
   "What happened to this person immediately before this picture?"
   "What will happen to this person immediately after this picture?"
   "What will happen to this person in the future?"
   "How does this person get along with other people?"
   "What does this person need most?"
   "What does that person make you think of?"
   "What does that person remind you of?"
   "How do you feel about that person?"
   "Do you feel that way about most people? Why?"

3. "What were you thinking about while you were drawing?"

4. "What does this drawing make you think of?"

5. Questions about the weather in the picture include:
   "What is the weather like in this picture?"
   "Is there any wind blowing in this picture?"
   "Show me the direction it is blowing?"
   "What sort of wind is it?"
   "If you had drawn a sun in this picture, where would you have put it?"

6. "What happened to this family/class in this picture immediately before this picture?"

7. "What will happen to this family/school in this picture immediately after this picture?"

8. "What will happen to this family/school in the future?"

9. "If you could change anything at all about this family/school picture, what would it be?"

10. "Is this the best picture that you could possibly make?"

**NOTES:**

## Sensorimotor Integration for Developmentally Disabled Children: A Handbook

Patricia Montgomery, Ph.D., RPT, and Eileen Richter, OTR

An important program that provides the occupational or physical therapist with useful, practical, and developmentally sequenced activities to improve sensory integrative functions.

Product No. W-142A

## Handbook of Psychological Signs, Symptoms, and Syndromes

Donald P. Ogdon, Ph.D.

This popular and well-organized text provides clinicians with a source for rapidly retrieving information for diagnosis and assessment of the common syndromes.

Product No. W-173

## House-Tree-Person Drawings: An Illustrated Diagnostic Handbook

L. Stanley Wenck, Ed.D.

With approximately 500 characteristics discussed and 183 examples illustrated, this comprehensive handbook is an essential reference for clinicians and students.

Product No. W-147

## Burks' Behavior Rating Scales Handbook, Revised: Diagnosis and Remediation of Learning and Behavior Problems

Harold F. Burks, Ph.D.

Structured around the 19 behavior disorders identified by the *Burks' Behavior Rating Scales,* this practitioner-oriented handbook will maximize the applicability of the BBRS.

Product No. W-148G

## Psychodiagnostics and Personality Assessment: A Handbook

Donald P. Ogdon, Ph.D.

An extremely popular reference dealing with the basic hypotheses for diagnosis and evaluation of personality with the most frequently used psychological tests.

Product No. W-95

## Mental Retardation Handbook

Martin N. Levine, Ed.D.

This handbook addresses the psychological evaluation of mentally retarded youngsters, specifically examining the tests commonly used to identify their needs and to assess their progress. It is a valuable resource for psychologists, special educators, and educational diagnosticians.

Product No. W-230

## Rorschach Introductory Guide

George Ulett, M.D.

Using this handy guide, you can quickly master the basics of *Rorschach* scoring and interpretation. Especially helpful to clinicians with limited training in psychological assessment, the *Rorschach Introductory Guide* makes it much easier to learn and use this popular projective tool.

Product No. W-285

## Interpretive Handbook for the Roberts Apperception Test for Children

Glen E. Roberts, Ph.D.

Here in one convenient handbook is the equivalent of a complete workshop on interpreting the popular *Roberts Apperception Test for Children* (RATC). Based on hundreds of clinical cases, plus new research on the use of projectives with children, this handbook clarifies scoring and interpretation, making the process quicker, easier, and more accurate.

Product No. W-288

## Assessment of Adolescent Alcohol and Drug Abuse: A Handbook

Ken C. Winters, Ph.D.

Written for practitioners, this useful handbook provides clear guidelines for assessing alcohol and drug problems in teenagers. Step-by-step, it takes you through the assessment process, showing how to select instruments, how and when to use them, and how to interpret and apply results.

Product No. W-291

## Attention Disorders in Children School-Based Assessment, Diagnosis, and Treatment

Richard Morriss, Ph.D.

This easy-to-understand handbook gives school practitioners the information they need to diagnose and treat ADD.

Product No. W-314A

## Handbook of Individualized Strategies for Classroom Discipline

George Selig, Ed.D., and Alan A. Arroyo, Ed.D.

Organized for quick reference, this handbook lets you look up a specific classroom problem and choose a discipline strategy that's not only appropriate for the problem but also compatible with the particular student's behavior style and level of maturation.

Product No. W-315A

Western Psychological Services ◆ 12031 Wilshire Boulevard ◆ Los Angeles, CA 90025-1251